I0661737

Wilhelm Wagner

A Book of Ballads on German History

Wilhelm Wagner

A Book of Ballads on German History

ISBN/EAN: 9783742899576

Manufactured in Europe, USA, Canada, Australia, Japa

Cover: Foto ©Thomas Meinert / pixelio.de

Manufactured and distributed by brebook publishing software (www.brebook.com)

Wilhelm Wagner

A Book of Ballads on German History

Pitt Press Series.

A

BOOK OF BALLADS

ON

GERMAN HISTORY.

ARRANGED AND ANNOTATED

BY

WILHELM WAGNER, Ph.D.

PROFESSOR AT THE JOHANNEUM, HAMBURG.

EDITED FOR THE SYNDICS OF THE UNIVERSITY PRESS.

Cambridge:

AT THE UNIVERSITY PRESS.

London: CAMBRIDGE WAREHOUSE, 17, Paternoster Row.
Cambridge: DEIGHTON, BELL, AND CO.

1877

PREFACE.

THE present Collection of Ballads on German History is an attempt to combine the study of German poetry with the history of the country. The Ballads have been arranged in chronological order, so as to form a series of historical poems from the earliest times down to the latest events. It is hoped that the plan of this work and the selection itself will meet with the approbation of experienced teachers. Not a little labour has been bestowed upon the commentary, in which both the subject-matter and the linguistic peculiarities of the ballads have been carefully elucidated. Besides the works referred to in the notes, the Editor has to acknowledge his obligations to the excellent collection edited by his colleague Dr Julius Bintz (*Ausgewählte Gedichte geschichtlichen Inhalts*, Leipzig, Teubner). He also begs to record his thanks to the learned editor of *The Missing Fragment of the Latin translation of the Fourth Book of Ezra*, Mr R. L. Bensly, to whom he owes many valuable hints and suggestions.

Hamburg, *November*, 1876.

CONTENTS.

I

Das Grab im Busento.

(410)

Nächtlich am Busento lispeln, bei Cosenza, dumpfe Lieder,
Aus den Wassern schallt es Antwort und in Wirbeln klingt
es wieder!
Und den Fluß hinauf — hinunter — ziehn die Schatten
tapfrer Gothen,
Die den Alarich beweinen, ihres Volkes besten Todten.
Allzufrüh und fern der Heimat mußten sie ihn hier be-
graben,   5
Während noch die Jugendlocken seine Schulter blond umgaben,
Und am Ufer des Busento reihten sie sich um die Wette;
Um die Strömung abzuleiten, gruben sie ein frisches Bette.
In der wogenleeren Höhlung wühlten sie empor die Erde,
Senkten tief hinein den Leichnam mit der Rüstung auf dem
Pferde,   10
Deckten dann mit Erde wieder ihn und seine stolze Habe,
Daß die hohen Stromgewächse wüchsen aus dem Heldengrabe.
Abgelenkt zum zweitenmale, ward der Fluß herbeigezogen;
Mächtig in ihr altes Bette schäumten die Busentowogen.
Und es sang ein Chor von Männern: „Schlaf in deinen
Heldenehren,   15

Keines Römers schnöde Habsucht soll dir je dein Grab versehren!
Sangen's, und die Lobgesänge tönten fort im Gothenheere!
Wälze sie, Busentowelle, wälze sie von Meer zu Meere.

August Graf von Platen.

2
Schlacht bei Zülpich.
(496)

Chlodewig, der Frankenkönig, sah in Zülpichs heißer Schlacht,
Daß die Alemannen siegten durch der Volkszahl Uebermacht.
Plötzlich aus des Kampf's Gedränge hebt er sich auf stolzem
    Roß,
Und man sah ihn herrlich ragen vor den Edlen, vor dem Troß.
Beide Arme, beide Hände hält er hoch empor zum Schwur, 5
Ruft mit seiner Eisenstimme, daß es durch die Reihen fuhr:
„Gott der Christen, Gott am Kreuze, Gott, den mein Gemahl
    verehrt,
So du bist ein Gott der Schlachten, der im Schrecken nieder-
    fährt,
Hilf mir dieses Volk bezwingen, gib den Sieg in meine Hand,
Daß der Franken Macht erkennen muß des Rheins, des
    Neckars Strand! 10
Sieh, so will ich an dich glauben, Kirchen und Kapellen bau'n,
Und die edlen Franken lehren, keinem Gott als dir vertrau'n."
Sprach es, und aus Wolken leuchtend bricht der Sonne voller
    Strahl,
Frischer Muth belebt die Herzen, füllt des schwachen Häufleins
    Zahl.
Chlodwig selbst ergriff das Banner, trug es in der Feinde
    Reih'n, 15

Und die Franken siegesmuthig stürzen jauchzend hinterdrein;
Schreck ergreift der Feinde Rotten, feige wenden sie und fliehn,
All ihr Kriegsruhm ist erloschen, ihre Macht und Freiheit hin.
König Chlodwig ließ sich taufen, und sein edles Volk zugleich,
Und vor allen deutschen Stämmen mächtig ward der Franken
    Reich. 20

Karl Simrock

3

Gelimer.

(534)

Wo ist dein Reich, o Gelimer,
Das große Vandalenreich?
Dein Heer, es irrt zerstreut umher;
Wo fliehst du hin so bleich?

Und als er zu den Maurusiern kam, 5
Die hatten nicht Brod, nicht Wein,
Wie man die Aehre vom Felde nahm,
So mußte sie Speise sein.

Auf einem Berge wohnet er,
Da war an Wasser Noth, 10
Auch nahete der Griechen Heer
Und drohte rings mit Tod.

Und einen Boten sandt' er hin
Zum Feind, als nah er kam,
Und bat um eine Laute ihn, 15
Um Brod und einen Schwamm.

Pharas, des Heeres Hüter, fragt:
„Sonst sprach er nichts dabei?

Er soll sie haben, aber sagt:
Wozu will er die Drei?" 20

Das Brod will essen Gelimer,
Weil keines er gesehn,
Seitdem mit wunden Füßen er
In die Berge mußte gehn.

Den Schwamm mit Wasser will er han 25
Zu waschen die Augen sein:
Es kam schon lange kein Wasser daran
Als seine Thränen allein.

Die Laute soll ein Trost ihm sein
In dieser schweren Zeit, 30
Drauf will er spielen und singen darein
Ein Lied von seinem Leid.

August Kopisch.

4

Pipin der Kurze.

(752)

Pipin der Kurze war nicht groß,
Doch Karls des Großen Vater,
In aller Weise fehlerlos,
Ein treuer Volksberather,

Der beste Held im Frankenreich, 5
Der Kirche Wohlgefallen,
An Weisheit nur sich selber gleich,
An Tapferkeit vor Allen.

War nicht geboren auf dem Thron,
Doch für den Thron geboren;   10
Zum Herrscher war des Hammers Sohn
Von Gottes Gnad' erkoren.

Papst Zacharias sprach dies Wort:
„Des Königs Würd' und Namen
Gebührt der Völker starkem Hort!"   15
Und alle Welt sprach: Amen!

Doch unser Held, der Kurze, schien
Zu klein manch kleinen Geistern,
Die maßen mit den Augen ihn,
Und hatten viel zu meistern.   20

Deß schwieg der Held, und ritterlich
Sinnt er den Hohn zu dämpfen,
Und ladt zum Spiele männiglich,
Wo wilde Thiere kämpfen.

Schon eilt das Volk herbei, mit Drang   25
Die stolzen Großen alle,
Sie nahen beim Trommetenklang,
Mit lautem Waffenschalle.

Still sitzt Pipin, gedankenschwer;
Wie nahend Ungewitter   30
Wirft er nur Blitze um sich her —
Da rauscht herab das Gitter.

Ein grimmer Leu, ein wilder Stier,
Die stürzen in die Schranken,
Begegnen sich mit Kampfbegier,   35
Und keiner wollte wanken.

Jetzt aber faßt des Leuen Zahn
Den Ur in dem Genicke,
Und reißt ihn nieder auf den Plan,
Blut, Feu'r und Wuth im Blicke.   40

„Wer ist von euch" — so fragt Pipin,
Und blitzet durch die Reihen —
„Wer ist von euch so stark und kühn,
Entreißt die Beut' dem Leuen?"

Da machen große Augen zwar   45
Ringsum die großen Leute;
Doch jeder bebt vor der Gefahr,
Und keiner will zum Streite.

Und wie noch Alle schweigend stehn
Und an dem Kampf verzagen,   50
Sieht man Pipin zum Kampfplatz gehn,
Allein den Strauß zu wagen.

Er ruft den blut'gen Löwen an
Mit donnergleicher Stimme;
Der stürzt auf ihn mit Wuth heran,   55
Und brüllt vor wildem Grimme.

Und alles Volk sieht es mit Graus,
Pipin nur ohne Grausen;
Sein gutes Schwert zur Scheid' heraus,
Läßt's durch die Lüfte sausen,   60

Und schlägt den Löwen in den Bart,
Daß todt er niederstürzet;
Das war ein Schlag nach Heldenart,
Mit Heldenkraft gewürzet.

Nun rafft der wilde Ur sich auf,   65
Den neuen Feind er wittert,
Und rennt heran in vollem Lauf,
Daß Schrank' und Boden zittert.

Doch unser Held steht mauerfest,
Und wankt nicht von der Stelle: 70
Das Schwert er wieder sausen läßt,
Und schwingt's mit Blitzesschnelle.

Und trifft den Schnaubenden so gut,
Dicht an des Nackens Rande —
Da spritzt zum Himmel schwarzes Blut,   75
Das Haupt stürzt hin zum Sande.

Wie nun, ihr großen Recken ihr,
Was dünkt euch von dem Kleinen?
Mag nun der Held im Kampfrevier
Euch groß genug erscheinen? —   80

Es stehn beschämt die Spötter werth,
Gesenkt die stolzen Blicke;
Pipin steckt ein sein gutes Schwert,
Dann tritt er schnell zurücke.

Des Volkes Jubel aber füllt   85
Ringsum die weiten Schranken;
Empor ihn hebend auf dem Schild
Zeigt ihn der Frank dem Franken.

Als König grüßt ihn alle Welt,
Die Spötter müssen schweigen,   90
Und ihm, der Leu und Ur gefällt,
Demüthiglich sich beugen.

Und Barden singen allzumal
Vom Stier- und Löwensturze;
Pipin glänzt in der Fürstenzahl: 95
Groß war Pipin der Kurze.

Baur.

5

Roland Schildträger.

(Roland † 778)

Der König Karl saß einst zu Tisch
Zu Aachen mit den Fürsten.
Man stellte Wildpret auf und Fisch
Und ließ auch keinen dürsten;
Viel Goldgeschirr von klarem Schein,   5
Manch rothen, grünen Edelstein
Sah man im Saale leuchten.

Da sprach Herr Karl, der starke Held:
„Was soll der eitle Schimmer?
Das beste Kleinod dieser Welt,   10
Das fehlet uns noch immer.
Dies Kleinod, hell wie Sonnenschein,
Ein Riese trägt's im Schilde sein,
Tief im Ardennerwalde."

Graf Richard, Erzbischof Turpin,   15
Herr Haimon, Naims von Baiern,
Milon von Anglant, Graf Garin,
Die wollten da nicht feiern;
Sie haben Stahlgewand begehrt
Und hießen satteln ihre Pferd',   20
Zu reiten nach dem Riesen.

Jung Roland, Sohn des Milon, sprach:
„Lieb Vater! hört, ich bitte!
Vermeint ihr mich zu jung und schwach,
Daß ich mit Riesen stritte,   25
Doch bin ich nicht zu winzig mehr,
Euch nachzutragen euern Speer
Samt eurem guten Schilde.“

Die sechs Genossen ritten bald
Vereint nach den Ardennen;   30
Doch als sie kamen in den Wald,
Da thäten sie sich trennen.
Roland ritt hinterm Vater her;
Wie wohl ihm wär, des Helden Speer,
Des Helden Schild zu tragen!   35

Bei Sonnenschein und Mondenlicht
Streiften die kühnen Degen;
Doch fanden sie den Riesen nicht
In Felsen noch Gehegen.
Zur Mittagsstund’ am vierten Tag   40
Der Herzog Milon schlafen lag
In einer Eiche Schatten.

Roland sah in der Ferne bald
Ein Blitzen und ein Leuchten,
Davon die Strahlen in dem Wald   45
Die Hirsch’ und Reh’ aufscheuchten;
Er sah, es kam von einem Schild,
Den trug ein Riese, groß und wild,
Vom Berge niedersteigend.

Roland gedacht’ im Herzen sein: 50
„Was ist das für ein Schrecken!

Soll ich den lieben Vater mein
Im besten Schlaf erwecken?
Es wachet ja sein gutes Pferd,
Es wacht sein Speer, sein Schild und Schwert,   55
Es wacht Roland, der junge."

Roland das Schwert zur Seite band,
Herrn Milons starkes Waffen,
Die Lanze nahm er in die Hand
Und thät den Schild aufraffen.   60
Herrn Milons Roß bestieg er dann
Und ritt ganz sachte durch den Tann,
Den Vater nicht zu wecken.

Und als er kam zur Felsenwand,
Da sprach der Ries' mit Lachen: 65
„Was will doch dieser kleine Fant
Auf solchem Rosse machen?
Sein Schwert ist zwar so lang als er,
Vom Rosse zieht ihn schier der Speer,
Der Schild will ihn erdrücken."   70

Jung Roland rief: „Wohlauf zum Streit!
Dich reuet noch dein Necken,
Hab' ich die Tartsche lang und breit,
Kann sie mich besser decken;
Ein kleiner Mann, ein großes Pferd,   75
Ein kurzer Arm, ein langes Schwert,
Muß eins dem andern helfen."

Der Riese mit der Stange schlug
Auslangend, in die Weite,
Jung Roland schwenkte schnell genug   80

Sein Roß noch auf die Seite.
Die Lanz' er auf den Riesen schwang,
Doch von dem Wunderschilde sprang
Auf Roland sie zurücke.

Jung Roland nahm in großer Hast   85
Das Schwert in beide Hände,
Der Riese nach dem seinen faßt,
Er war zu unbehende;
Mit flinkem Hiebe schlug Roland
Ihm unterm Schild die linke Hand,   90
Daß Hand und Schild entrollten.

Dem Riesen schwand der Muth dahin,
Wie ihm der Schild entrissen,
Das Kleinod, das ihm Kraft verliehn,
Mußt' er mit Schmerzen missen.   95
Zwar lief er gleich dem Schilde nach,
Doch Roland in das Knie ihn stach,
Daß er zu Boden stürzte.

Roland ihn bei den Haaren griff,
Hieb ihm das Haupt herunter,   100
Ein großer Strom von Blute lief
Ins tiefe Thal hinunter,
Und aus des Todten Schild hernach
Roland das lichte Kleinod brach,
Und freute sich am Glanze.   105

Dann barg er's unterm Kleide gut
Und ging zu einem Quelle,
Da wusch er sich von Staub und Blut
Gewand und Waffen helle.

B.   2

Zurücke ritt der jung' Roland   110
Dahin, wo er den Vater fand,
Noch schlafend bei der Eiche.

Er legt' sich an des Vaters Seit',
Vom Schlafe selbst bezwungen,
Bis in der kühlen Abendzeit   115
Herr Milon aufgesprungen:
„Wach' auf, wach' auf, mein Sohn Roland!
Nimm Schild und Lanze schnell zur Hand,
Daß wir den Riesen suchen!"

Sie stiegen auf und eilten sehr,   120
Zu schweifen in der Wilde,
Roland ritt hinterm Vater her
Mit dessen Speer und Schilde.
Sie kamen bald zu jener Stätt',
Wo Roland jüngst gestritten hätt',   125
Der Riese lag im Blute.

Roland kaum seinen Augen glaubt,
Als nicht mehr war zu schauen
Die linke Hand, dazu das Haupt,
So er ihm abgehauen,   130
Nicht mehr des Riesen Schwert und Speer,
Auch nicht sein Schild und Harnisch mehr,
Nur Rumpf und blut'ge Glieder.

Milon besah den großen Rumpf:
„Was ist das für 'ne Leiche?   135
Man sieht noch am zerhaunen Stumpf,
Wie mächtig war die Eiche.
Das ist der Riese, frag' ich mehr?

Verschlafen hab' ich Sieg und Ehr',
Drum muß ich ewig trauren."   140

Zu Aachen vor dem Schlosse stund
Der König Karl gar bange:
"Sind meine Helden wohl gesund?
Sie weilen allzu lange.
Doch seh' ich recht, auf Königswort!   145
So reitet Herzog Haimon dort,
Des Riesen Haupt am Speere."

Herr Haimon ritt in trübem Muth,
Und mit gesenktem Spieße
Legt' er das Haupt, besprengt mit Blut,   150
Dem König vor die Füße;
"Ich fand den Kopf im wilden Hag,
Und fünfzig Schritte weiter lag
Des Riesen Rumpf am Boden."

Bald auch der Erzbischof Turpin   155
Den Riesenhandschuh brachte,
Die ungefüge Hand noch drin,
Er zog sie aus und lachte:
"Das ist ein schön Reliquienstück,
Ich bring' es aus dem Wald zurück,   160
Fand es schon zugehauen."

Der Herzog Naims von Baierland
Kam mit des Riesen Stange:
"Schaut an, was ich im Walde fand!
Ein Waffen, stark und lange.   165
Wohl schwitz' ich von dem schweren Druck,
Hei! bairisch Bier, ein guter Schluck,
Sollt' mir gar köstlich munden!"

Graf Richard kam zu Fuß daher,
Ging neben seinem Pferde,   170
Das trug des Riesen schwere Wehr,
Den Harnisch samt dem Schwerte:
„Wer suchen will im wilden Tann,
Manch Waffenstück noch finden kann,
Ist mir zu viel gewesen."   175

Der Graf Garin thät ferne schon
Den Schild des Riesen schwingen:
„Der hat den Schild, deß ist die Kron',
Der wird das Kleinod bringen!"
„Den Schild hab' ich, ihr lieben Herrn!   180
Das Kleinod hätt' ich gar zu gern,
Doch das ist ausgebrochen."

Zuletzt thät man Herrn Milon sehn,
Der nach dem Schlosse lenkte,
Er ließ das Rößlein langsam gehn,   185
Das Haupt er traurig senkte.
Roland ritt hinterm Vater her
Und trug ihm seinen starken Speer
Zusammt dem festen Schilde.

Doch wie sie kamen vor das Schloß   190
Und zu den Herrn geritten,
Macht' er von Vaters Schilde los
Den Zierrath in der Mitten;
Das Riesenkleinod setzt' er ein,
Das gab so wunderklaren Schein,   195
Als wie die liebe Sonne.

Und als nun diese helle Glut
Im Schilde Milons brannte,

Da rief der König frohgemuth:
„Heil Milon von Anglante!   200
Der hat den Riesen übermannt,
Ihm abgeschlagen Haupt und Hand,
Das Kleinod ihm entrissen."

  Herr Milon hatte sich gewandt,
Sah staunend all' die Helle: 205
„Roland! sag an, du junger Fant!
Wer gab dir das, Geselle?"
„Um Gott, Herr Vater, zürnt mir nicht,
Daß ich erschlug den groben Wicht,
Derweil Ihr eben schliefet!"   210

Uhland.

6

Die Sage von Wittekind.

(785)

Da kaum die Hügel matt erhellte
Der morgenrothe, lichte Schein,
Wer schleicht sich in die Zelte
Des Frankenlagers ein?
Mit Schritten leise, leise,   5
Wie Späherschritte sind,
Verfolgt er die geheime Reise;
Das ist der Sachse Wittekind.

Schon focht er wider muth'ge Franken
Durch lange Jahre blut'gen Streit,   10
Und grollte sonder Wanken
Dem Herrn der Christenheit;

Nun schlich er kühn und schnelle
Zum Feinde sich bei Nacht,
Vertauschend seine Heldenfelle   15
Mit einer feigen Bettlertracht.

Da fühlt er plötzlich sich umrungen
Von Melodien sanft und weich,
Gesungen wird, geklungen
Wird um ihn her zugleich.   20
Verwundert eilt er weiter,
Durchzieht das rüst'ge Heer,
Da sieht er Beter statt der Streiter,
Das Kreuz als ihre ganze Wehr.

Weihnachten war herangekommen,   25
Der heil'ge Morgen war erglüht,
Und innig schwoll des frommen,
Des großen Karls Gemüth;
Zum hohen Tempelbaue
Ließ wölben er sein Zelt,   30
Daß er im Land der Heiden schaue
Die Glorie der Christenwelt.

Hoch überm Altar prangt und raget
Ein blauer, golddurchwirkter Thron,
Drauf sitzt die reine Maged   35
Und ihr im Schooß der Sohn.
Hell schimmert rings das schöne,
Das heilige Geräth,
Und alle Farben, alle Töne
Begrüßen sich mit Majestät.   40

Schon kniete brünstig, stillanbächtig
Der Kaiser vor dem Hochaltar,

Mit Grafenkronen prächtig
Um ihn die Heldenschaar;
Schon fällt vom Spiel der Lichter   45
Ein rosenfarbner Schein
Auf ihre klaren Angesichter;
Da tritt der Heide keck hinein.

Er staunt, als er die stolzen Päre
Mit Karl auf ihren Knien erkennt,   50
Damit sie himmlisch nähre
Das ew'ge Sakrament;
Doch staunt er deß nicht minder,
Was man dem Gotte bot:
Nicht Pferde fielen hier, noch Rinder,   55
Sie opferten nur Wein und Brot.

Der Priester bot zum Liebesmahle
Die Hostie dem Kaiser dar,
Die auf smaragdner Schale
Sich wandelt wunderbar;   60
Was alles Volk erquickte
Unter des Brotes Bild,
Ein lebend Kind darin erblickte
Sein Aug', ein Knäblein süß und mild.

Er sieht das schöne Kind erlachen,   65
Ihm freundlich winken: „Komm zu mir;
Ich will dich glücklich machen,
Und selig dort und hier."
Und Jubel füllt die Seelen,
Empfahend Brot und Wein,   70
Es bringt ein Lied aus tausend Kehlen
Von göttlichem Zugegensein.

Der Sachse steht betäubt, er faltet
Die Hände fromm, sein Aug' ist naß,
Das hohe Wunder spaltet   75
Den heidnisch argen Haß.
Hin eilt er, wo der Haufe
Mit frohem Blick ihn mißt:
„Gib, Karl, dem Wittekind die Taufe,
Daß er umarme dich als Christ."   80

Platen.

(Strophe 7, 8, 9 von Simrock.)

7

Ludwig des Frommen Tod.

(20. Juni 840)

Es kommt ein Schiff geschwommen
Herab den stolzen Rhein,
Die weißen Segel wallen
Im goldnen Mittagsschein;
Umgeben von Getreuen   5
Ruht drin gebettet weich
Der fromme Kaiser Ludwig
So krank und todesbleich.

„Legt an, legt an, ihr Schiffer,
Bei dieser stillen Au,   10
Da wehn durch schatt'ge Bäume
Die Lüfte mild und lau;
Da rasseln keine Schwerter,
Da tönt kein Schlachtgesang
Mir vom Verrath der Söhne   15
Den fürchterlichen Klang."

„Und auf dem grünen Rasen,
Ihr Treuen, spannt mein Zelt,
Auf daß in Frieden ruhe
Der Herrscher einer Welt.   20
Schon rauscht des Rheines Welle
Ein sanftes Schlummerlied,
Und leichter wird sich schließen
Mein Auge trüb und müd."

Es sprach's der kranke Kaiser,   25
Da wird erfüllt sein Wort,
Man trägt ihn auf ein Lager
Am kleinen Inselport.
Wie blaß sind seine Wangen,
Wie todesmatt sein Blick,   30
Er richtet ihn voll Trauer
Nach Ingelheim zurück.

Und auf den Zinnen leuchtet
Der letzte Abendstrahl,
Die hundert Säulen schimmern   35
Am stolzen Kaisersaal;
Da fühlt der fromme Ludwig,
Daß seine Stunde schlägt,
Er betet lang und leise
Und sagt, von Schmerz bewegt: 40

„Seht, wie der Glanz der Säulen
Verschwunden ist in Nacht,
Bald wird auch so vergehen
Der Karolinger Macht! —
Sagt meinen fernen Söhnen,   45
In Wehr und Waffen wild,

Daß sie das Herz gebrochen,
Zu weich und vatermild."

„Doch will es gern vergeben,
Vergessen muß es bald   50
Der Erde Lust und Schmerzen,
Haß, Liebe und Gewalt!
Ihr Ritter, nehmt die Krone,
Umglänzt von flücht'gem Schein,
Lothar soll sie empfangen,   55
Er wird nun Kaiser sein."

„Und bringt ihm auch den Scepter,
Zu schwer oft meiner Hand,
Bringt ihm den Purpurmantel,
Mir gnügt ein Sterbgewand.   60
Denn nun zum brittenmale
Vom stolzen Kaiserthron,
Doch ach, ins Grab hernieder
Steigt, großer Karl, dein Sohn."

„Aus — aus" — sein Auge sinket,   65
Umhüllt von Todesnacht,
Er hat den Kampf bestanden,
Er hat den Sieg vollbracht.
Und um die Königsleiche
Knie'n traurig und voll Schmerz   70
Die Ritter zum Gebete
Für das gebrochne Herz.

Adelheid von Stolterfoth.

8

Heinrich der Finkler.

(919)

Herr Heinrich sitzt am Vogelherd
Recht froh und wohlgemuth;
Aus tausend Perlen blinkt und blitzt
Der Morgenröthe Glut.

In Wies' und Feld und Wald und Au —   5
Horch, welch ein süßer Schall!
Der Lerche Sang, der Wachtel Schlag,
Die süße Nachtigall!

Herr Heinrich schaut so fröhlich drein:
„Wie schön ist heut die Welt!   10
Was gilt's? heut gibt's 'nen guten Fang!"
Er lugt zum Himmelszelt.

Er lauscht und streicht sich von der Stirn
Das blondgelockte Haar:
„Ei doch! was sprengt denn dort herauf   15
Für eine Reiterschaar?"

Der Staub wallt auf, der Hufschlag dröhnt,
Es naht der Waffen Klang.
„Daß Gott! die Herrn verderben mir
Den ganzen Vogelfang!"   20

„Ei nun! Was gibt's?" — Es hält der Troß
Vor'm Herzog plötzlich an;
Herr Heinrich tritt hervor und spricht:
„Wen sucht ihr Herrn? sagt an!"

Da schwenken sie die Fähnlein bunt 25
Und jauchzen: „Unsern Herrn! —
Hoch lebe König Heinrich! — Hoch
Des Sachsenlandes Stern!" —

Dies rufend knie'n sie vor ihn hin
Und huldigen ihm still 30
Und rufen, als er staunend fragt:
„'s ist deutschen Reiches Will'!"

Da blickt Herr Heinrich tiefbewegt
Hinauf zum Himmelszelt:
„Du gabst mir einen guten Fang, 35
Herr Gott, wie Dir's gefällt."

Vogl.

9

Kaiser Otto I.

(942)

Zu Quedlinburg im Dome ertönet Glockenklang,
Der Orgel Stimmen brausen zum ernsten Chorgesang:
Es sitzt der Kaiser drinnen mit seiner Ritter Macht,
Voll Andacht zu begehen die heil'ge Weihenacht.

Hoch ragt er in dem Kreise, von männlicher Gestalt, 5
Das Auge scharf wie Blitze, von goldnem Haar umwallt;
Man hat ihn nicht zum Scherze den Löwen nur genannt,
Schon Mancher hat empfunden die löwenstarke Hand.

Wohl ist auch jetzt vom Siege er wieder heimgekehrt,
Doch nicht des Reiches Feinden hat mächtig er gewehrt; 10
Es ist der eigne Bruder, den seine Waffe schlug,
Der dreimal der Empörung blutrothes Banner trug.

Jetzt schweift er durch die Lande geächtet, flüchtig hin,
Das will dem edlen Kaiser gar schmerzlich in den Sinn;
Er hat die schlimme Fehde oft bitter schon beweint: 15
„O Heinrich, du mein Bruder, was bist du mir so feind!"

Zu Quedlinburg vom Dome ertönt die Mitternacht,
Vom Priester wird das Opfer der Messe dargebracht,
Es beugen sich die Kniee, es beugt sich jedes Herz,
Gebet in heil'ger Stunde steigt brünstig himmelwärts.   20

Da öffnen sich die Pforten, es tritt ein Mann herein,
Es hüllt die starken Glieder ein Büßerhemde ein —
Er schreitet auf den Kaiser, er wirft sich vor ihm hin,
Die Knie' er ihm umfasset mit tiefgebeugtem Sinn.

„O Bruder, meine Fehle, sie lasten schwer auf mir;   25
Hier liege ich zu Füßen, Verzeihung flehend, dir;
Was ich mit Blut gesündigt, die Gnade macht es rein,
Vergib, vergib, o Kaiser, vergib, du Bruder mein!"

Doch strenge blickt der Kaiser den sünd'gen Bruder an:
„Zweimal hab' ich vergeben: nicht fürder mehr fortan!
Die Acht ist ausgesprochen, das Leben dir geraubt,   31
Nach dreier Tage Wechsel, da fällt dein schuldig Haupt!"

Bleich werden rings die Fürsten, der Herzog Heinrich bleich,
Und Stille herrscht im Kreise, gleich wie im Todtenreich,
Man hätte mögen hören jetzt wohl ein fallend Laub,   35
Denn Keiner wagt zu wehren dem Löwen seinen Raub.

Da hat sich ernst zum Kaiser der fromme Abt gewandt,
Das ew'ge Buch der Bücher, das hält er in der Hand;
Er liest mit lautem Munde der heil'gen Worte Klang,
Daß es in Aller Herzen wie Gottesstimme drang.   40

„Und Petrus sprach zum Herren: Nicht so? Genügt ich hab',
Wenn ich dem sünb'gen Bruder schon siebenmal vergab?
Doch Jesus ihm antwortet: Nicht siebenmal vergib,
Nein, siebenzig mal sieben, das ist dem Vater lieb."

Da schmilzt des Kaisers Strenge in Thränen unbewußt, 45
Er hebt ihn auf, den Bruder, er drückt ihn an die Brust;
Ein lauter Ruf der Freude ist jubelnd rings erwacht,
Nie schöner ward begangen die heil'ge Weihenacht.

Heinr. v. Mühler.

10

Klaglied Kaiser Ottos III.

(1002)

O Erde, nimm den Müden,
Den Lebensmüden auf,
Der hier im fernen Süden
Beschließt den Pilgerlauf!
Schon steh' ich an der Grenze,   5
Die Leib und Seele theilt,
Und meine zwanzig Lenze
Sind rasch dahingeeilt.

Voll unerfüllter Träume,
Verwaist, in Gram versenkt,   10
Entfallen mir die Zäume,
Die dieses Reich gelenkt.
Ein Andrer mag es zügeln
Mit Händen minder schlaff,
Von diesen sieben Hügeln   15
Bis an des Nordens Haff.

Doch selbst im Seelenreiche
Harrt meiner noch die Schmach;
Es folgt der blassen Leiche
Begangner Frevel nach: 20
Vergebens mit Gebeten
Beschwör' ich diesen Bann,
Und mir entgegen treten
Crescentius und Johann.

Doch nein! die Stolzen beugte   25
Mein reuemüthig Flehn;
Ihn, welcher mich erzeugte,
Ihn werd' ich wiedersehn!
Nach welchem ich als Knabe
So oft vergebens frug: 30
An seinem frühen Grabe
Hab' ich geweint genug.

Des deutschen Volks Berather
Umwandeln Gottes Thron;
Mir winkt der Aeltervater   35
Mit seinem großen Sohn;
Und während voll von Milde
Die frommen Hände legt
Mir auf das Haupt Mathilde,
Steht Heinrich tief bewegt.   40

Nun fühl' ich erst, wie eitel
Des Glücks Geschenke sind,
Wiewohl ich auf dem Scheitel
Schon Kronen trug als Kind!
Was je mir schien gewichtig,   45
Zerstiebt wie ein Atom:

O Welt, du biſt ſo nichtig,
Du biſt ſo klein, o Rom!

O Rom, wo meine Blüthen
Verwelkt, wie dürres Laub,   50
Dir ziemt es nicht, zu hüten
Den kaiſerlichen Staub!
Die mir die Treue brachen,
Zerbrächen mein Gebein:
Beim großen Karl in Aachen   55
Will ich beſtattet ſein.

Die echten Palmen wehen
Nur dort um ſein Panier:
Ihn hab' ich liegen ſehen,
In ſeiner Kaiſerzier.   60
Was durfte mich verführen,
Zu öffnen ſeinen Sarg?
Den Lorbeer anzurühren,
Der ſeine Schläfe barg?

O Freunde, laßt das Klagen,   65
Mir aber gebt Entſatz,
Und macht dem Leichenwagen
Mit euern Waffen Platz!
Bedeckt das Grab mit Roſen,
Das ich ſo früh gewann,   70
Und legt den thatenloſen
Zum thatenreichſten Mann!

        Platen.

II

Kaiser Heinrich II.

(1002—1024)

Herzog Heinrich war's von Bayern,
Der sich in der Mitternacht,
Wo die frömmsten Brüder feiern,
Hin zur Kirche aufgemacht.
Ernste Bilder nach ihm fassen,   5
Treiben ihn zum Beten an,
Durch die Regensburger Gassen
Geht er nach Sanct Heimeran.

Junges Heldenantlitz betend
Möcht' ein schöner Anblick sein;   10
Dieser, zum Altare tretend,
Kniet umnachtet und allein.
Vor den Augen gar die Hände,
Drückend jedes Bild zurück,
Fleht er um ein sel'ges Ende,   15
Nicht um irdisch Heil und Glück.

Als er aufstand, schien's vom Rücken
Ueber ihn, als wie ein Licht;
Staunend thät er um sich blicken,
Sieht ein heil'ges Angesicht.   20
Hochaltar und Kreuz verklärend
Dort ein lichter Bischof stand,
Der mit hoher Hand, wie schwörend,
Zeigte nach der Kirchenwand.

Mit den Fingern, wie mit Kerzen,   25
Leuchtet er auf eine Schrift,

Wo der Fürst mit bangem Herzen
Auf ein' röm'sche Sechse trifft.
„Will mich Gott so bald erhören?
Herr, ich glaub's auf eure Hand,   30
Hebt sie nicht so ernst zum Schwören!"
Sprach der Held, und Alles schwand.

Wie sechs Stunden sind vergangen,
Harrt er fromm auf seinen Tod,
Doch es schien ihm auf die Wangen   35
Lebenshell das Morgenroth.
Wie der sechste Tag gekommen,
Er bereit und fertig ist,
Doch es gibt der Herr dem Frommen
Neue heit're Lebensfrist.   40

Darum hält er an mit Beten,
Bis der sechste Mond erscheint,
Würd'ger stets vor Gott zu treten —
Doch es war nicht so gemeint.
Aber ernste Todsgedanken   45
Wandeln mit ihm immerdar,
Und so lebt er sonder Wanken
Heilig bis in's sechste Jahr.

Und in hoher Kirche stand er
Leuchtend um das sechste Jahr,   50
Und auf seinem Haupte fand er
Röm'sche Königskrone gar.
König Heinrich war's, der Zweite,
Herr von allem deutschen Land,
Der von dort an ward bis heute   55
Stets der Heilige genannt.

Zwei und zwanzig Jahre heilig
Herrſcht' er ohne Fluch und Spott;
An die röm'ſche Sechſe treulich
Dacht' er und an Tod und Gott.   60
Weil er fertig war zum Sterben,
Hielt ihn Gott des Lebens werth,
Weil den Himmel er konnt' erben,
Ward ihm auch das Reich beſcheert.

Guſtav Schwab.

12

Die Weiber von Weinsberg.

(1140)

Der erſte Hohenſtaufe, der König Konrad, lag
Mit Heeresmacht vor Weinsberg ſeit manchem langen Tag;
Der Welfe war geſchlagen, noch wehrte ſich das Neſt,
Die unverzagten Städter, die hielten es noch feſt.

Der Hunger kam, der Hunger!   Das iſt ein ſcharfer Dorn.
Nun ſuchten ſie die Gnade, nun fanden ſie den Zorn: 6
„Ihr habt mir hier erſchlagen gar manchen Degen werth,
Und öffnet ihr die Thore, ſo trifft euch doch das Schwert."

Da ſind die Weiber kommen: „Und muß es alſo ſein,
Gewährt uns freien Abzug, wir ſind vom Blute rein!"   10
Da hat ſich vor den Armen des Helden Zorn gekühlt,
Da hat ein ſanft Erbarmen im Herzen er gefühlt.

„Die Weiber mögen abziehn, und jede habe frei,
Was ſie vermag zu tragen und ihr das Liebſte ſei;
Laßt ziehn mit ihrer Bürde ſie ungehindert fort,   15
Das iſt des Königs Meinung, das iſt des Königs Wort."

3—2

Und als der frühe Morgen im Osten kaum gegraut,
Da hat ein seltnes Schauspiel vom Lager man geschaut;
Es öffnet leise, leise sich das bedrängte Thor,
Es schwankt ein Zug von Weibern mit schwerem Tritt hervor.

Tief beugt die Last sie nieder, die auf dem Nacken ruht,   21
Sie tragen ihre Ehherrn, das ist ihr liebstes Gut.
„Halt an die argen Weiber!" ruft drohend mancher Wicht;
Der Kanzler spricht bedeutsam: „Das war die Meinung nicht."

Da hat, wie er's vernommen, der fromme Herr gelacht: 25
„Und war es nicht die Meinung, sie haben's gut gemacht:
Gesprochen ist gesprochen, das Königswort besteht,
Und zwar von keinem Kanzler zerdeutelt und zerbreht."

So war das Gold der Krone wohl rein und unentweiht.
Die Sage schallt herüber aus halb vergeßner Zeit.   30
Im Jahr elfhundertvierzig, wie ich's verzeichnet fand,
Galt Königswort noch heilig im deutschen Vaterland.

Adalbert von Chamisso.

13

Schwäbische Kunde.

(1190)

Als Kaiser Rothbart lobesam
Zum heil'gen Land gezogen kam,
Da mußt' er mit dem frommen Heer
Durch ein Gebirge, wüst und leer.
Daselbst erhub sich große Noth,   5
Viel Steine gab's und wenig Brot,
Und mancher deutsche Reitersmann
Hat dort den Trunk sich abgethan.

Den Pferden war's so schwach im Magen,
Fast mußt' der Reiter die Mähre tragen.   10
Nun war ein Herr aus Schwabenland,
Von hohem Wuchs und starker Hand,
Deß Rößlein war so krank und schwach,
Er zog es nur am Zaume nach,
Er hätt' es nimmer aufgegeben   15
Und kostet's ihn das eigne Leben.
So blieb er bald ein gutes Stück
Hinter dem Heereszug zurück.
Da sprengten plötzlich in die Quer
Funfzig türkische Reiter daher,   20
Die huben an, auf ihn zu schießen,
Nach ihm zu werfen mit den Spießen.
Der wackre Schwabe forcht sich nit,
Ging seines Weges Schritt vor Schritt,
Ließ sich den Schild mit Pfeilen spicken   25
Und thät nur spöttlich um sich blicken,
Bis Einer, dem die Zeit zu lang,
Auf ihn den krummen Säbel schwang.
Da wallt dem Deutschen auch sein Blut,
Er trifft des Türken Pferd so gut,   30
Er haut ihm ab mit Einem Streich
Die beiden Vorderfüß' zugleich.
Als er das Thier zu Fall gebracht,
Da faßt er erst sein Schwert mit Macht;
Er schwingt es auf des Reiters Kopf,   35
Haut durch bis auf den Sattelknopf,
Haut auch den Sattel noch in Stücken,
Und tief noch in des Pferdes Rücken;
Zur Rechten sieht man, wie zur Linken,
Einen halben Türken heruntersinken.   40

Da packt die Andern kalter Graus,
Sie fliehen in alle Welt hinaus,
Und Jedem iſt's, als würd' ihm mitten
Durch Kopf und Leib hindurchgeſchnitten.
Drauf kam des Wegs 'ne Chriſtenſchaar,   45
Die auch zurückgeblieben war,
Die ſahen nun mit gutem Bedacht,
Was Arbeit unſer Held gemacht.
Von denen hat's der Kaiſer vernommen,
Der ließ den Schwaben vor ſich kommen,   50
Er ſprach: „Sag' an, mein Ritter werth!
Wer hat dich ſolche Streich' gelehrt?"
Der Held bedacht' ſich nicht zu lang:
„Die Streiche ſind bei uns im Schwang,
Sie ſind bekannt im ganzen Reiche,   55
Man nennt ſie halt nur Schwabenſtreiche."
                                         Uhland.

14

Barbarossa.

(+ 1190)

Der alte Barbaroſſa,
Der Kaiſer Friederich,
Im unterird'ſchen Schloſſe
Hält er verzaubert ſich.

Er iſt niemals geſtorben,   5
Er lebt darin noch jetzt,
Er hat im Schloß verborgen
Zum Schlaf ſich hingeſetzt.

Er hat hinabgenommen
Des Reiches Herrlichkeit   10

Und wird einst wiederkommen
Mit ihr, zu seiner Zeit.

Der Stuhl ist elfenbeinern,
Darauf der Kaiser sitzt;
Der Tisch ist marmelsteinern,   15
Worauf sein Haupt er stützt.

Sein Bart ist nicht von Flachse,
Er ist von Feuersglut,
Ist durch den Tisch gewachsen,
Worauf sein Kinn ausruht.   20

Er nickt als wie im Traume,
Sein Aug' halb offen zwinkt;
Und je nach langem Raume
Er einem Knaben winkt.

Er spricht im Schlaf zum Knaben: 25
„Geh' hin vor's Schloß, o Zwerg,
Und sieh, ob noch die Raben
Herfliegen um den Berg!

Und wenn die alten Raben
Noch fliegen immerdar,   30
So muß ich auch noch schlafen
Verzaubert hundert Jahr'."

Rückert.

15

Der Schenk von Limburg.

Zu Limburg auf der Feste,
Da wohnt' ein edler Graf,
Den keiner seiner Gäste
Jemals zu Hause traf.

Er trieb sich allerwegen   5
Gebirg und Wald entlang,
Kein Sturm und auch kein Regen
Verleidet' ihm den Gang.

Er trug ein Wams von Leder
Und einen Jägerhut   10
Mit mancher wilden Feder;
Das steht den Jägern gut.
Es hing ihm an der Seiten
Ein Trinkgefäß von Buchs;
Gewaltig konnt' er schreiten,   15
Und war von hohem Wuchs.

Wohl hatt' er Knecht' und Mannen
Und hatt' ein tüchtig Roß,
Ging doch zu Fuß von dannen,
Und ließ daheim den Troß.   20
Es war sein ganz Geleite
Ein Jagdspieß, stark und lang,
An dem er über breite
Waldströme kühn sich schwang.

Nun hielt auf Hohenstaufen   25
Der deutsche Kaiser Haus.
Der zog mit hellen Haufen
Einstmals zu jagen aus.
Er rannt' auf eine Hinde
So heiß und hastig vor,   30
Daß ihn sein Jagdgesinde
Im wilden Forst verlor.

Bei einer kühlen Quelle
Da macht' er endlich Halt;

Gezieret war die Stelle   35
Mit Blumen mannigfalt.
Hier dacht' er sich zu legen
Zu einem Mittagsschlaf,
Da rauscht' es in den Hägen,
Und stand vor ihm der Graf.   40

Da hub er an zu schelten:
„Treff' ich den Nachbar hie?
Zu Hause weilt er selten,
Zu Hofe kömmt er nie:
Man muß im Walde streifen,   45
Wenn man ihn sahen will,
Man muß ihn tapfer greifen,
Sonst hält er nirgend still."

Als drauf ohn' alle Fährde
Der Graf sich niederließ,   50
Und neben in die Erde
Die Jägerstange stieß,
Da griff mit beiden Händen
Der Kaiser nach dem Schaft:
„Den Spieß muß ich mir pfänden,   55
Ich nehm' ihn mir zur Haft.

Der Spieß ist mir verfangen,
Deß ich so lang begehrt,
Du sollst dafür empfangen
Hier dies mein bestes Pferd.   60
Nicht schweifen im Gewälde
Darf mir ein solcher Mann,
Der mir zu Hof und Felde
Viel besser dienen kann."

„Herr Kaiser, wollt vergeben!   65
Ihr macht das Herz mir schwer.
Laßt mir mein freies Leben,
Und laßt mir meinen Speer!
Ein Pferd hab' ich schon eigen,
Für eures sag' ich Dank;   70
Zu Rosse will ich steigen,
Bin ich mal alt und krank."

„Mit dir ist nicht zu streiten,
Du bist mir allzu stolz;
Doch führst du an der Seiten   75
Ein Trinkgefäß von Holz;
Nun macht die Jagd mich dürsten,
Drum thu mir das, Gesell,
Und gib mir eins zu bürsten
Aus diesem Wasserquell."   80

Der Graf hat sich erhoben,
Er schwenkt den Becher klar,
Er füllt ihn an bis oben,
Hält ihn dem Kaiser dar.
Der schlürft mit vollen Zügen   85
Den kühlen Trank hinein,
Und zeigt ein solch Vergnügen,
Als wär's der beste Wein.

Dann faßt der schlaue Zecher
Den Grafen bei der Hand: 90
„Du schwenktest mir den Becher
Und fülltest ihn zum Rand;
Du hieltest mir zum Munde
Das labende Getränk:

Du bist von dieser Stunde   95
Des deutschen Reiches Schenk!"
Uhland.

16

König Enzio's Tod.

(1272)

„O König, schöner König
Mit deinem goldnen Haar,
Mit deinen blauen Augen,
Gefangner stolzer Aar!
Wie Renos Welle schallet   5
Dein Lied so lustig und frei;
Im Kerker und in Banden
Bricht nicht dein Herz entzwei?" —

„Im Kerker und in Banden
Blieb Lust und Hoffen mir treu,   10
Und ob sie den Leib mir umwanden
Mit Ketten, die Seele blieb frei.
Noch leuchtet am Himmel die Sonne,
Die Sterne, sie glänzen noch hell,
Noch trägt mein Vater die Krone,   15
Der rettet, der rettet mich schnell." —

„O König, schöner König,
Wirf Lust und Hoffen ins Meer!
Die Sonne leuchtet am Himmel,
Die goldene Sonne nicht mehr!   20
Laß alle Schleusen springen
Des Schmerzes blutigroth!
Dein Vater ist gestorben,
Der Kaiser, der Kaiser ist todt." —

„Und ist mein Vater gestorben,   25
Der große Friedrich todt,
So sei sie Gott geklaget,
Des Reichs und meine Noth!
Zehn Monde will ich klagen
Ein großes, tiefes Leid,   30
Zehn Monde will ich tragen
Ein schwarzes Trauerkleid.

Die Vögel will ich lehren
Meines Schmerzes Melodien,
Die Wogen sollen klagend   35
Nach meinen Weisen ziehn.
Doch locket der Frühling wieder
Die Klänge der Lust herfür:
Noch glänzen am Himmel die Sterne,
Noch leben die Brüder mir." —   40

„O König, schöner König,
Wirf Lust und Hoffen ins Meer!
Die Sterne, die glänzen am Himmel,
Die hellen Sterne nicht mehr.
Die Brüder sind gefallen   45
In heißer, blutiger Schlacht;
Du bist die letzte Trümmer
Von deines Hauses Pracht." —

„Und sind gestürzt aus den Höhen
Die Sterne so feurig und klar,   50
So will ich mit Staub mich besäen,
Mit Asche dies goldene Haar.
Wie ein Sohn um seine Mutter,

Ums Kind die Nachtigall,
Will in blutigen Thränen ich klagen   55
Um meines Hauses Fall.

Doch wird's auf den Auen lustig
Und schallet der Vögel Gesang,
So hall' im Thurm auch wieder
Aufs neue der Freude Klang!   60
Mein Vater stieg in den Himmel,
Die Brüder sanken ins Grab;
Doch Freund und Harf' und Liebe,
Das ist's, was ich noch hab'.

Zwei Sonnen, der Liebsten Augen,   65
Sie schmücken das Kerkerhaus
Mit himmlisch hellen Strahlen
Zum Königssaal mir aus.
Des Freundes Muth verschönet
Den Bund beim rosigen Wein,   70
Und lustiges Harfenspiel tönet
Ins blühende Land hinein." —

„O König, schöner König,
Wirf Lust und Hoffen ins Meer!
Ich sah sie gestern begraben,   75
Dein Herzlieb ist nicht mehr.
Im Unglück dein heitrer Geselle,
Der treue Freund ist todt;
Heut' Nacht hat er verblutet
Für dich auf dem Schaffot."   80

„Und ist mein Herzlieb gestorben
Und hat verblutet die Treu',

Das könnt' ein Herz wohl brechen,
Das Herz im Leib entzwei.
Den Vater, die Brüder, die Liebe,   85
Den Freund verschlang das Grab,
So bist du, Harfe, mein Alles,
Was ich im Leib noch hab'!

Zur Klage will ich dich stimmen,
Daß bleich die Sonne scheint,   90
Daß Mond und Stern' erblinden
Und Ros' und Lilie weint.
Und zwischen die Klagen web' ich
Die alten Lieder hinein,
Daß mich die Geister umschweben   95
Der Herzallerliebsten mein.

Die alten lustigen Lieder,
Sie seien die goldene Brück',
Die trage mein weißes Liebchen
Ans heiße Herz mir zurück!   100
Die alten lustigen Lieder,
Die rufen als Glockengeläut
Den lieben Freund aus dem Grabe,
Die alte fröhliche Zeit." —

„O König, schöner König,   105
Wirf Lust und Hoffen ins Meer!
In diesen Mauern schallet
Kein Klang der Saiten mehr.
Die Harfe, die heitere Seele,
Die woll'n sie zerschlagen dir: 110
Einsam in der Kerkerhöhle
Vertrauern sollst du hinfür." —

„Und woll'n sie die Harf' mir zerschlagen,
Fahr wohl denn, Lust und Schmerz!
So mögen sie mich begraben,   115
Sie haben gebrochen mein Herz!
Mein Herz und meine Harfe,
So singt eu'r Schwanenlied!
Ade, du schöne Erde!
Der letzte Staufe schied."   120

                    B. F. W. Zimmermann.

17

Der Graf von Habsburg.

(1273)

Zu Aachen in seiner Kaiserpracht,
Im alterthümlichen Saale,
Saß König Rudolfs heilige Macht
Beim festlichen Krönungsmahle.
Die Speisen trug der Pfalzgraf des Rheins,   5
Es schenkte der Böhme des perlenden Weins,
Und alle die Wähler, die sieben,
Wie der Sterne Chor um die Sonne sich stellt,
Umstanden geschäftig den Herrscher der Welt,
Die Würde des Amtes zu üben.   10

Und rings erfüllte den hohen Balkon
Das Volk in freud'gem Gedränge,
Laut mischte sich in der Posaunen Ton
Das jauchzende Rufen der Menge;
Denn geendigt nach langem verderblichem Streit   15
War die kaiserlose, die schreckliche Zeit,

Und ein Richter war wieder auf Erden.
Nicht blind mehr waltet der eiserne Speer,
Nicht fürchtet der Schwache, der Friedliche mehr,
Des Mächtigen Beute zu werden.   20

Und der Kaiser ergreift den goldnen Pokal
Und spricht mit zufriedenen Blicken:
„Wohl glänzet das Fest, wohl pranget das Mahl,
Mein königlich Herz zu entzücken;
Doch den Sänger vermiss' ich, den Bringer der Lust, 25
Der mit süßem Klang mir bewege die Brust
Und mit göttlich erhabenen Lehren.
So hab' ich's gehalten von Jugend an,
Und was ich als Ritter gepflegt und gethan,
Nicht will ich's als Kaiser entbehren."   30

Und sieh! in der Fürsten umgebenden Kreis
Trat der Sänger im langen Talare;
Ihm glänzte die Locke silberweiß,
Gebleicht von der Fülle der Jahre.
„Süßer Wohllaut schläft in der Saiten Gold,   35
Der Sänger singt von der Minne Sold,
Er preiset das Höchste, das Beste,
Was das Herz sich wünscht, was der Sinn begehrt;
Doch sage, was ist des Kaisers werth
An seinem herrlichsten Feste?"   40

„Nicht gebieten werd' ich dem Sänger," spricht
Der Herrscher mit lächelndem Munde,
„Er steht in des größeren Herren Pflicht,
Er gehorcht der gebietenden Stunde.
Wie in den Lüften der Sturmwind saust,   45
Man weiß nicht, von wannen er kommt und braust,

Wie der Quell aus verborgenen Tiefen,
So des Sängers Lied aus dem Innern schallt,
Und weckt der dunkeln Gefühle Gewalt,
Die im Herzen wunderbar schliefen." 50

Und der Sänger rasch in die Saiten fällt
Und beginnt sie mächtig zu schlagen:
„Aufs Waidwerk hinaus ritt ein edler Held,
Den flüchtigen Gemsbock zu jagen.
Ihm folgte der Knapp' mit dem Jägergeschoß, 55
Und als er auf seinem stattlichen Roß
In eine Au kommt geritten,
Ein Glöcklein hört er erklingen fern,
Ein Priester wars mit dem Leib des Herrn,
Voran kam der Meßner geschritten. 60

Und der Graf zur Erde sich neiget hin,
Das Haupt mit Demuth entblößet,
Zu verehren mit gläubigem Christensinn,
Was alle Menschen erlöset.
Ein Bächlein aber rauschte durchs Feld, 65
Von des Gießbachs reißenden Fluten geschwellt,
Das hemmte der Wanderer Tritte,
Und beiseit legt jener das Sakrament,
Von den Füßen zieht er die Schuhe behend,
Damit er das Bächlein durchschritte. 70

„Was schaffst du?" redet der Graf ihn an,
Der ihn verwundert betrachtet.—
„Herr, ich walle zu einem sterbenden Mann,
Der nach der Himmelskost schmachtet;
Und da ich mich nahe des Baches Steg, 75
Da hat ihn der strömende Gießbach hinweg

Im Strubel der Wellen geriſſen.
Drum daß dem Lechzenden werde ſein Heil,
So will ich das Wäſſerlein jetzt in Eil'
Durchwaten mit nackenden Füßen."   80

Da ſetzt ihn der Graf auf ſein ritterlich Pferd
Und reicht ihm die prächtigen Zäume,
Daß er labe den Kranken, der ſein begehrt,
Und die heilige Pflicht nicht verſäume.
Und er ſelber auf ſeines Knappen Thier   85
Vergnüget noch weiter des Jagens Begier;
Der Andre die Reiſe vollführet;
Und am nächſten Morgen, mit dankendem Blick,
Da bringt er dem Grafen ſein Roß zurück,
Beſcheiden am Zügel geführet.   90

„Nicht wolle das Gott," rief mit Demuthſinn
Der Graf, „daß zum Streiten und Jagen
Das Roß ich beſchritte fürderhin,
Das meinen Schöpfer getragen!
Und magſt du's nicht haben zu eignem Gewinnſt,   95
So bleibt es gewidmet dem göttlichen Dienſt:
Denn ich hab' es Dem ja gegeben,
Von dem ich Ehre und irdiſches Gut
Zu Lehen trage, und Leib und Blut
Und Seele und Athem und Leben."   100

„So mög' euch Gott, der allmächtige Hort,
Der das Flehen der Schwachen erhöret,
Zu Ehren euch bringen hier und dort,
So wie ihr jetzt ihn geehret.
Ihr ſeid ein mächtiger Graf, bekannt   105
Durch ritterlich Walten im Schweizerland,

Euch blühn sechs liebliche Töchter.
So mögen sie, rief er begeistert aus,
Sechs Kronen euch bringen in euer Haus
Und glänzen die spätsten Geschlechter!"   110

Und mit sinnendem Haupt saß der Kaiser da,
Als dächt' er vergangener Zeiten;
Jetzt, da er dem Sänger ins Auge sah,
Da ergreift ihn der Worte Bedeuten.
Die Züge des Priesters erkennt er schnell,   115
Und verbirgt der Thränen stürzenden Quell
In des Mantels purpurnen Falten.
Und Alles blickte den Kaiser an,
Und erkannte den Grafen, der das gethan,
Und verehrte das göttliche Walten.   120

Schiller.

18

Kaiser Rudolfs Ritt zum Grabe.

(1291)

Auf der Burg zu Germersheim,
　　Stark am Geist, am Leibe schwach,
Sitzt der greise Kaiser Rudolf,
　　Spielend das gewohnte Schach.

Und er spricht: „Ihr guten Meister!   5
　　Aerzte! sagt mir ohne Zagen:
Wann aus dem zerbrochnen Leib
　　Wird der Geist zu Gott getragen?"

Und die Meister sprechen: „Herr,
　　Wohl noch heut erscheint die Stunde."   10

4—2

Freundlich lächelnd spricht der Greis:
„Meister! Dank für diese Kunde!"

„Auf nach Speier, auf nach Speier!"
Ruft er, als das Spiel geendet;
„Wo so mancher deutsche Held
Liegt begraben, sei's vollendet!

Blast die Hörner! bringt das Roß,
Das mich oft zur Schlacht getragen!"
Zaudernd stehn die Diener all;
Doch er ruft: „Folgt ohne Zagen!"

Und das Schlachtroß wird gebracht.
„Nicht zum Kampf, zum ew'gen Frieden,"
Spricht er, „trage, treuer Freund,
Jetzt den Herrn, den lebensmüden!"

Weinend steht der Diener Schaar,
Als der Greis auf hohem Rosse,
Rechts und links ein Kapellan,
Zieht, halb Leich', aus seinem Schlosse.

Trauernd neigt des Schlosses Lind'
Vor ihm ihre Aeste nieder,
Vögel, die in ihrer Hut,
Singen wehmuthsvolle Lieder.

Mancher eilt des Wegs daher,
Der gehört die bange Sage,
Sieht des Helden sterbend Bild,
Und bricht aus in laute Klage.

Aber nur von Himmelslust
Spricht der Greis mit jenen zweien,

Lächelnd blickt sein Angesicht,
Als ritt' er zur Lust im Maien.   40

Von dem hohen Dom zu Speier
Hört man dumpf die Glocken schallen.
Ritter, Bürger, zarte Frau'n
Weinend ihm entgegenwallen.

In den hohen Kaisersaal   45
Ist er rasch noch eingetreten;
Sitzend dort auf goldnem Stuhl,
Hört man für sein Volk ihn beten.

„Reichet mir den heil'gen Leib!"
Spricht er dann mit bleichem Munde;   50
Drauf verjüngt sich sein Gesicht
Um die mitternächt'ge Stunde.

Da auf einmal wird der Saal
Hell von überird'schem Lichte,
Und entschlummert sitzt der Held,   55
Himmelsruh' im Angesichte.

Glocken dürfen's nicht verkünden,
Boten nicht zur Leiche bieten,
Alle Herzen längs des Rheins
Fühlen, daß der Held verschieden.   60

Nach dem Dome strömt das Volk,
Schwarz, unzähligen Gewimmels.
Der empfing des Helden Leib,
Seinen Geist der Dom des Himmels.

                                   Justinus Kerner.

19

Der Landgraf von Thüringen.

(1307)

Der edle Landgraf Friederich
Mit der gebißnen Wange
Auf seiner Wartburg ritterlich
Sich wehrt und schirmet lange.

In seinen Adern heiß ihm rollt   5
Das Blut der Hohenstaufen.
Darum ihm Papst und Habsburg grollt,
Die ihm das Land verkaufen.

Der Kaiser Albrecht, Rudolfs Sohn,
Zertritt die deutschen Lande,   10
Fügt zu dem Unrecht kalten Hohn
Und zu dem Elend Schande.

Die Wartburg, auf den Fels erhöht,
Die kann er nicht gewinnen,
Der edlen Freiheit Wiege steht   15
In ihren stolzen Zinnen.

Doch droht des Hungers Uebermacht
Die Burg zu übermannen.
Drum führt der Landgraf still bei Nacht
Die Seinigen von bannen.   20

Sie reiten über Stock und Stein,
Zu fliehn des Kaisers Ketten.
Der Landgraf denket nur allein
Sein liebes Kind zu retten.

Er trägt ihn selbst auf seinem Arm,   25
Den Knaben neugeboren;
Vom starken Ritt wird ihm so warm,
Schon bluten ihm die Sporen.

„Fort, fort! dort weht das Reichspanier,
Schon blinken tausend Speere.   30
Der Kaiser ist's, voll blut'ger Gier,
Mit seinem ganzen Heere!"

Und wären's mehr, als Sand am Meer,
Der Landgraf wird's nicht achten.
Sein kleines Kind, es weint so sehr,   35
Und will vor Durst verschmachten.

Vor einem schlechten Bauernhaus
Ruft er: „Um Gotteswillen
Du junge Mutter, komm' heraus,
Den Knaben mir zu stillen!"   40

Derweil umwendet er sein Pferd
Mit grimmen Zornesflammen,
Und wo er hinschlägt mit dem Schwert,
Stürzt Mann und Roß zusammen.

Die Seinen schaaren voller Wuth   45
Sich um den edlen Helden,
Daß von dem hier vergoßnen Blut
Noch späte Sagen melden.

Denn mehr als tausend Feinde sind
Hier in den Tod gesunken,   50
Bis sich des Landgrafs junges Kind
Hat ruhig satt getrunken.

                              Wolfgang Menzel.

20

Die Schlacht bei Reutlingen.
(Mai 1377)

Zu Achalm auf dem Felsen, da haust manch kühner Aar,
Graf Ulrich, Sohn des Greiners, mit seiner Ritterschaar;
Wild rauschen ihre Flügel um Reutlingen, die Stadt,
Bald scheint sie zu erliegen, vom heißen Drange matt.

Doch plötzlich einst erheben die Städter sich zu Nacht,   5
Ins Urachthal hinüber sind sie mit großer Macht,
Bald steigt von Dorf und Mühle die Flamme blutigroth,
Die Heerden weggetrieben, die Hirten liegen todt.

Herr Ulrich hat's vernommen, er ruft im grimmen Zorn:
„In eure Stadt soll kommen kein Huf und auch kein
        Horn!"   10
Da sputen sich die Ritter, sie wappnen sich in Stahl,
Sie heischen ihre Rosse, sie reiten stracks zuthal.

Ein Kirchlein stehet brunten, Sankt Leonhard geweiht,
Dabei ein grüner Anger, der scheint bequem zum Streit.
Sie springen von den Pferden, sie ziehen stolze Reih'n,   15
Die langen Spieße starren, wohlauf! wer wagt sich drein?

Schon ziehn vom Urachthale die Städter fern herbei,
Man hört der Männer Jauchzen, der Heerden wild Geschrei,
Man sieht sie fürder schreiten, ein wohlgerüstet Heer;
Wie flattern stolz die Banner! Wie blitzen Schwert und
        Speer!   20

Nun schließ dich fest zusammen, du ritterliche Schaar!
Wohl hast du nicht geahnet so dräuende Gefahr.

Die übermächt'gen Rotten, sie stürmen an mit Schwall,
Die Ritter stehn und starren wie Fels und Mauerwall.

Zu Reutlingen am Zwinger, da ist ein altes Thor,　25
Längst wob mit dichten Ranken der Epheu sich davor,
Man hat es schier vergessen, nun kracht's mit einmal auf,
Und aus dem Zwinger stürzet, gedrängt, ein Bürgerhauf'.

Den Rittern in den Rücken fällt er mit grauser Wuth,
Heut will der Städter baden im heißen Ritterblut.　30
Wie haben da die Gerber so meisterlich gegerbt!
Wie haben da die Färber so purpurroth gefärbt!

Heut nimmt man nicht gefangen, heut geht es auf den Tod,
Heut spritzt das Blut wie Regen, der Anger blümt sich roth.
Stets drängender umschlossen und wüthender bestürmt,　35
Ist rings von Bruderleichen die Ritterschaar umthürmt.

Das Fähnlein ist verloren, Herr Ulrich blutet stark,
Die noch am Leben blieben, sind müde bis ins Mark.
Da haschen sie nach Rossen und schwingen sich darauf,
Sie hauen durch, sie kommen zur festen Burg hinauf.　40

„Ach Allm"—stöhnt' einst ein Ritter, ihn traf des Mörders
　　　Stoß —
Allmächt'ger! wollt' er rufen — man hieß davon das Schloß.
Herr Ulrich sinkt vom Sattel, halbtodt, voll Blut und Qualm,
Hätt' nicht das Schloß den Namen, man hieß es jetzt:
　　　Achalm.

Wohl kommt am andern Morgen zu Reutlingen ans Thor　45
Manch trauervoller Knappe, der seinen Herrn verlor.
Dort auf dem Rathhaus liegen die Todten all gereiht,
Man führt dahin die Knechte. mit sicherem Geleit.

Dort liegen mehr denn sechzig, so blutig und so bleich,
Nicht jeder Knapp erkennet den todten Herrn sogleich. 50
Dann wird ein jeder Leichnam von treuen Dieners Hand
Gewaschen und gekleidet in weißes Grabgewand.

Auf Bahren und auf Wagen, getragen und geführt,
Mit Eichenlaub bekränzet, wie's Helden wohl gebührt,
So geht es nach dem Thore, die alte Stadt entlang, 55
Dumpf tönet von den Thürmen der Todtenglocken Klang.

Götz Weißenheim eröffnet den langen Leichenzug,
Er war es, der im Streite des Grafen Banner trug;
Er hatt' es nicht gelassen, bis er erschlagen war,
Drum mag er würdig führen auch noch die todte Schaar. 60

Drei edle Grafen folgen, bewährt im Schildesamt,
Von Tübingen, von Zollern, von Schwarzenberg entstammt.
O Zollern! deine Leiche umschwebt ein lichter Kranz:
Sahst du vielleicht noch sterbend dein Haus im künft'gen
        Glanz?

Von Sachsenheim zween Ritter, der Vater und der Sohn, 65
Die liegen still beisammen in Lilien und in Mohn,
Auf ihrer Stammburg wandelt von Alters her ein Geist,
Der längst mit Klaggeberden auf schweres Unheil weist.

Einst war ein Herr von Lustnau vom Scheintod aufer-
        wacht,
Er kehrt im Leichentuche zu seiner Frau bei Nacht, 70
Davon man sein Geschlechte die Todten hieß im Scherz;
Hier bringt man ihrer Einen, den traf der Tod ins Herz.

Das Lied, es folgt nicht weiter, des Jammers ist genug,
Will Jemand Alle wissen, die man von bannen trug,

Dort auf den Rathhausfenstern, in Farben bunt und klar, 75
Stellt jeden Ritters Name und Wappenschild sich dar.

Als nun von seinen Wunden Graf Ulrich ausgeheilt,
Da reitet er nach Stuttgart, er hat nicht sehr geeilt;
Er trifft den alten Vater allein am Mittagsmahl,
Ein frostiger Willkommen! kein Wort ertönt im Saal. 80

Dem Vater gegenüber sitzt Ulrich an dem Tisch,
Er schlägt die Augen nieder, man bringt ihm Wein und
　　Fisch;
Da faßt der Greis ein Messer, und spricht kein Wort dabei,
Und schneidet zwischen Beiden das Tafeltuch entzwei.

Uhland.

21

Der reichste Fürst.

(1495)

Preisend mit viel schönen Reden
Ihrer Länder Werth und Zahl,
Saßen viele deutsche Fürsten
Einst zu Worms im Kaisersaal.

„Herrlich," sprach der Fürst von Sachsen,　　　　　5
„Ist mein Land und seine Macht,
Silber hegen seine Berge
Wohl in manchem tiefen Schacht."

„Seht mein Land in üpp'ger Fülle,"
Sprach der Pfalzgraf von dem Rhein,　　　　　10
„Goldne Saaten in den Thälern,
Auf den Bergen edlen Wein."

„Große Städte, reiche Klöster,"
Ludwig, Herr zu Baiern, sprach,
„Schaffen, daß mein Land den euren   15
Wohl nicht steht an Schätzen nach."

Eberhard, der mit dem Barte,
Würtembergs geliebter Herr,
Sprach: „Mein Land hat kleine Städte,
Trägt nicht Berge silberschwer;   20

Doch ein Kleinod hält's verborgen:
Daß in Wäldern, noch so groß,
Ich mein Haupt kann kühnlich legen
Jedem Unterthan in Schooß."

Und es rief der Herr von Sachsen,   25
Der von Baiern, der vom Rhein:
„Graf im Bart! Ihr seid der reichste,
Euer Land trägt Edelstein!"

Justinus Kerner.

22

Kaiser Max zu Worms.

(1495)

Zur Gruft sank Kaiser Friedrich. Gott geb' ihm sanfte Ruh!
Max faßt sein gülden Scepter; ei, Sonnenaar, Glück zu!
Zu Worms nun hielt er Reichstag; auf, Fürstenschaar,
     herbei,
Zu rathen und zu fördern, daß Recht und Licht gedeih'!

Einst in dem dumpfen Rathsaal sprang Max empor in
    Hast,   5
Der Staub der Pergamente nahm ihm den Odem fast,
Die spitzen klugen Reden, die machten toll ihn schier,
Da rief er seinen Narren: „Freund Kunze, komm mit mir!"

Den Treu'n liebt er vor Allen, wohl einem Gärtner gleich,
Der jeden Baum mit Liebe pflegt in dem Gartenreich, 10
Doch einen sich erkoren, in dessen Schattenhut
Nach schwüler Tagesmüh' er am liebsten abends ruht.

Es wallten nun die Beiden die Straßen ein und aus,
Dort auf dem großen Marktplatz sahn sie ein stattlich Haus,
Da rief der Kunz: „Mein König, schließt Eure Augen
    schnell!   15
Denn, traun, schon las manch einer sich blind an dieser
    Stell'.

Französisch ist's; Ihr wißt ja, wie's Frankreichs Söhne
    treiben,
Die anders schreiben als sprechen, und anders lesen als
    schreiben,
Und anders sprechen als denken, und anders setzen als singen,
Die groß in allem Kleinen, und klein in großen Dingen." 20

Ein Rittersmann aus Frankreich wohnt in dem stolzen
    Haus,
Sein Wappenschild, hell glänzend, hängt hoch zur Pfort'
    hinaus,
Mit Schnörkelzügen zierlich in blankem Goldesschein
Schrieb rings ums bunte Wappen er diese Worte ein:

„Erst Gott zum Gruß, wer's liefet! — Auf, Deutscher, kühn
 und werth,   25
Hier harrt ein Schild des deinen, wenn kampfesfroh dein
 Schwert,
Und magst du mich bezwingen nach Ritterbrauch und Recht,
Will ich mich dir verdingen als letzten Rübenknecht."

Ernst schritt der König fürder; doch an des Ritters Schild
Hängt bald ein Edelknappe der Habsburg Wappenbild;   30
Und mit dem Frühroth harrte auf sand'gem Kampfesplan
Der König gegenüber dem fränk'schen Rittersmann.

Und höher stieg die Sonne; der Franzmann lag im Sand,
Das Siegesschwert, hell leuchtend, ragt hoch in Marens
 Hand.
„So schlägt ein deutscher Ritter"; er sprach's und stand
 verklärt,   35
Wie Sanct Michael, der Sieger, mit seinem Flammenschwert.

„Ihr habt Euch mir ergeben als letzten Rübenknecht,
Wohlan, Ihr sollt erfahren nun meines Amtes Recht!"
Sein Schwert nun schwang er dreimal: „Steht auf, mein
 Ritter werth!
So schlägt ein deutscher König, — seid brav wie Euer
 Schwert!"   40

                *   *   *   *   *   *

Viel saft'ge Trauben schwellen ringsher um Worms am
 Rhein,
„Milch unsrer lieben Frauen," so heißt dort jener Wein;
Saugt jene Milch, ihr Greise, sie macht euch wieder zum
 Kind,
O Herr, gib unserm Lande viel Milch so süß und lind!

Aus Goldgefäßen quoll sie an Marens Abendtisch,   45
Gleichwie aus goldnen Eutern, so labend, klar und frisch;
Wie zecht an Marens Seite der fränk'sche Rittersmann!
Wie wärmend da der Glühborn durch Kunzens Kehle rann!

Der Franzmann hob den Becher, begeistert flammt sein Blut:
„Heil Max dir, edler Deutscher, so bieder und so gut!"   50
„Hoho!" rief Kunz halbgrimmig, „jetzt bindet mit mir an,
Wer auf dies Wohl herzinn'ger und besser trinken kann!"

Wie Schilde klangen die Becher zusammen jetzt mit Macht,
Die Blicke blitzten genüber, wie Lanzen in der Schlacht.
Wer Sieger blieb im Wettkampf? wohl kam es nie ans
        Licht;   55
Frug man am Morgen die Beiden, sie wußten's selber nicht.

                          Anastasius Grün.

                          23

Luther und Frundsberg.

(17. April 1521)

Schon harret an den Thüren
Des Volkes Menge dicht,
Als sie den Luther führen
Vor Kaiser und Gericht;
Und an der Thüre Pfosten,   5
Dem Eingang Luthers nah,
Steht fest auf seinem Posten
Der alte Frundsberg da.

Wie unter Blitzesflammen,
Wie unter Sturmeswehn   10

Zwei Eichen dicht beisammen
Auf zähen Wurzeln stehn,
So stehen kühngestaltig
Die beiden Helden dort,
In Waffen der gewaltig   15
Und jener in dem Wort.

Den schirmt die Pickelhaube,
Das Panzerhemd aus Erz,
Und jenem stählt der Glaube
Das vielgeprüfte Herz;   20
In Schlachten schaut der Eine
Dem Tod ins Angesicht,
Dem zittern die Gebeine
Auch vor dem Teufel nicht.

Der Ritter sieht den Priester   25
Sich werfen in den Tod,
In seinen Zügen liest er
Der Losung ernst Gebot,
Das siegen oder sterben
Den Frommverwegnen heißt,   30
Und vor dem Himmelserben
Beugt sich des Helden Geist.

„Mönchlein!" beginnt der Ritter,
„Du gehest einen Gang,
Wie auch im Schlachtgewitter,   35
Im Mord= und Sturmesdrang
Ich noch bestanden keinen
Und keinen werb' bestehn;
Bist du mit Gott im Reinen,
Magst du den Gang auch gehn!"   40

So gab der greise Degen
Am heißen Kampfestag
Dem Luther seinen Segen,
Den Hand- und Ritterschlag.
Wohlauf denn, Held! und schwinge 45
Dein ritterliches Schwert!
Laß sehn, ob sich die Klinge
Als flammende bewährt!

K. R. Hagenbach.

24

Kaiser Karl an Luthers Grab.

(1547)

In Wittenberg, der starken Luthersfeste,
Ist Kaiser Karl, der Sieger, eingedrungen.
Wohl ist den Stamm zu fällen ihm gelungen,
Doch neue Wurzeln schlagen rings die Aeste.

In Luthers Feste hausen fremde Gäste, 5
Doch Luthers Geist, der bleibet unbezwungen;
Da, wo des Geistes Schwert er hat geschwungen,
Da ruhen billig auch des Leibes Reste.

Am Grabe steht der Kaiser, tief gerührt.
„Auf denn und räche dich an den Gebeinen, 10
Den Flammen gib sie preis, wie sich's gebühret!"
So hört man aus der Diener Troß den Einen.
Der Kaiser spricht: „Den Krieg hab' ich geführet
Mit Lebenden; um Todte laßt uns weinen."

Hagenbach.

B. 5

25

Der Pilgrim vor St. Just.

(1557)

Nacht ist's, und Stürme sausen für und für:
Hispanische Mönche, schließt mir auf die Thür!
Laßt hier mich ruh'n, bis Glockenton mich weckt,
Der zum Gebet euch in die Kirche schreckt!
Bereitet mir, was euer Haus vermag,
Ein Ordenskleid und einen Sarkophag!
Gönnt mir die kleine Zelle, weiht mich ein!
Mehr als die Hälfte dieser Welt war mein.
Das Haupt, das nun der Scheere sich bequemt,
Mit mancher Krone war's bediademt.
Die Schulter, die der Kutte nun sich bückt,
Hat kaiserlicher Hermelin geschmückt.
Nun bin ich vor dem Tod den Todten gleich,
Und fall' in Trümmer, wie das alte Reich.

Platen.

26

Wallenstein vor Stralsund.

(1629)

Im Schatten einer Eiche
Ist Frieblands Zelt erbaut;
Es schüttelt ihre Zweige
Die alte Riesin laut.

Umhüllt vom Purpurkleide,
Im Zelt der Herzog sitzt;

Viel goldenes Geschmeide
An Hals und Brust ihm blitzt.

Doch finster hat zur Erde
Sein Auge sich gewandt;   10
Die Rechte mit dem Schwerte
Durchgräbt des Bodens Sand.

Es sitzet ihm zur Seite
Arnim, der Feldmarschall;
Deß Blick schweift in die Weite   15
Hin nach der Festung Wall.

Er spricht: „Nun selbst erfahren
Habt Ihr der Bürger Muth!
Geschützt sind vor Gefahren
Sie durch der Ostsee Flut!"   20

„Könnt Ihr der Feinde Flotte
Nicht bohren in den Grund,
So steht zu ihrem Spotte
Noch lang' Ihr vor Stralsund!"

Da hebt von seinem Sitze   25
Sich Friedland stolz empor,
Ihm sprühn des Zornes Blitze
Aus dunklem Auge vor.

„Es schleudert in die Fluten
Den Dänen diese Hand!   30
Den Schweden jagt mit Ruthen
Sie aus dem deutschen Land!"

„Bei Gott! Stralsund erretten
Soll keine Macht der Welt,

Und hing' es auch mit Ketten
Fest an dem Himmelszelt!"

Der Herzog ruft's im Grimme;
Da rauscht und ächzt zugleich
Es schaurig, wie die Stimme
Der Geister, im Gezweig.

Er hört's und schauet düster
Nach dem Geräusch empor,
Bis es, ein leis Geflüster,
Im Baume sich verlor.

Mit fragender Geberde
Blickt ihn der Marschall an;
Der Herzog sah zur Erde,
Bis lachend er begann:

„Was ist's! Die Winde brausen!"
Er greift in Hast zum Wein,
Und schenkt mit innerm Grausen
Für sich und Arnim ein.

„Stoßt an und laßt uns trinken!
Es gilt der Festung Fall!
In Kurzem soll sie sinken
Trotz Meeresflut und Wall!"

Die Becher sind erklungen
In der erhobnen Hand,
Und Frieblands Glas, zersprungen,
Fiel klirrend in den Sand.

Mit fragender Geberde
Blickt ihn der Marschall an;

Der Herzog sah zur Erde,
Bis lachend er begann:

„Was ist's! Ich stieß zu heftig!   65
Bringt Gläser uns herbei!"
Ein Diener holt geschäftig
Der frischen Becher zwei.

„Stoßt an! Wir müssen trinken
Auf dieser Festung Fall,   70
Und morgen soll sie sinken!
Stoßt an, Herr Feldmarschall!"

Anstießen sie bedächtig;
Es klang so hell und rein,
Und bei dem Klange mächtig   75
Auflachte Wallenstein.

Doch oben durch die Eiche
Rauscht es wie Geisterton,
Als sprächen alle Zweige
Dem Schwur des Herzogs Hohn.   80

Und sieh! der Festung Wälle
Umzuckt' es, Blitz auf Blitz,
Und seine Eisenbälle
Entsandte das Geschütz.

Der Herzog an die Lippen   85
Setzt schon des Bechers Rand;
Doch eh' er konnte nippen,
Entfuhr das Glas der Hand.

Des Weines Tropfen spritzten
Um Kinn und Bart und Mund,   90

Des Bechers Scherben ritzten
Die blasse Wang' ihm wund.

Und der noch nie gezittert
In heißer Schlachten Glut,
Ein Glas, vom Schuß zersplittert,   95
Brach ihm den kecken Muth.

Mit fragender Geberde
Blickt ihn der Marschall an;
Der Herzog sah zur Erde,
Bis düster er begann: 100

„Mit Menschen wollt' ich fechten
Und hoffte Ruhm und Sieg,
Doch mit des Schicksals Mächten
Führt Friedland nimmer Krieg!"

„Abziehn wir von der Feste,   105
Sobald der Morgen graut!"
Da rauscht es durch die Aeste
Wie heller Jubellaut.

Noch steht die Herzogseiche.
Da sammelt jedes Jahr   110
Im Schatten ihrer Zweige
Sich froh der Bürger Schaar.

Fr. Günther.

27
Fehrbellin.
(28. Juni 1675)

Herr Kurfürst Friedrich Wilhelm, der große Kriegesheld,
Seht, wie er auf dem Schimmel vor den Geschützen hält!

Das war ein rasches Reiten vom Rhein bis an den Rhin,
Das war ein heißes Streiten am Tag von Fehrbellin.

Wollt ihr, ihr trotz'gen Schweden, noch mehr vom deutschen
    Land? 5
Was tragt ihr in die Marken den wüth'gen Kriegesbrand?
Herr Ludwig von der Seine, der hat euch aufgehetzt,
Daß Deutschland von der Peene zum Elsaß werd' zersetzt.

Doch nein, Graf Gustav Wrangel, hier steh' nun einmal still!
Dort kommt Herr Friedrich Wilhelm, der mit dir reden
    will. 10
Gesellschaft aller Arten bringt er im raschen Ritt
Samt Fahnen und Standarten zur Unterhaltung mit.

Nun seht ihn auf dem Schimmel, ein Kriegsgott ist er traun!
Den Boden dort zum Tanze will er genau beschaun;
Und unter seinen Treuen da reitet hintenan 15
Zuletzt, doch nicht aus Scheuen, Stallmeister Froben an.

Und wie Herr Wrangel drüben den Schimmel nun erblickt,
Ruft er den Kanonieren: „Ihr Kinder, zielt geschickt!
Der auf dem Schimmel sitzet, der große Kurfürst ist's.
Nun donnert und nun blitzet, auf wen's geschieht, ihr
    wißt's!" 20

Die donnern und die blitzen und zielen wohl nichts Schlecht's,
Und um den Herren fallen die Seinen links und rechts.
Dem Dörflinger, dem Alten, fast wird es ihm zu warm;
Er ist kein Freund vom Halten mit dem Gewehr im Arm.

Und dicht und immer dichter schlägt in die Heeresreih'n 25
Dort in des Schimmels Nähe der Kugelregen ein.

„Um Gott, Herr Kurfürst, weichet!" Der Kurfürst hört es
    nicht;
Es schaut sein Blick, der gleiche, dem Feind in's Angesicht.

Der Schimmel mocht' es ahnen, wem dieses Feuer gilt;
Er steigt und schäumt im Zügel, er hebt sich scheu und
    wild.   30
Die Herren alle bangen, doch sagt's ihm keiner an;
Wär' doch nicht rückwärts gangen, der fürstlich große Mann.

O Preußen, damals wägte auf eines Auges Blick,
Auf eines Zolles Breite sich furchtbar dein Geschick!
O Zollern, deine Krone, o Friederich, dein Ruhm!   35
Hier galt's im Ahn dem Sohne, im Hut dem Königthum.

Hier galt es Sieg und Freiheit ob nord'scher Uebermacht,
Und wer, wenn er gefallen, wer schlüge seine Schlacht?
Nicht Homburgs edle Hitze, nicht Dörflings rauher Muth,
Nicht Grumbkows Säbelspitze, nicht Heer noch Landsturm
    gut.   40

Und doch, der Tod ist nahe und mäht um ihn herum,
Und Alles zagt und trauert und Alles bleibet stumm.
Die Scheibe ist der Schimmel, das merket Jeder nun;
Doch helfen mag der Himmel, von uns kann's Keiner thun.

Da reitet zu dem Fürsten Emanuel Froben her: 45
„Herr Kurfürst, Euer Schimmel, er scheut sich vor'm Gewehr;
Das Thier zeigt seine Launen, Ihr bringt's nicht in's Gefecht,
So nehmt nur meinen Braunen, ich reit's indeß zurecht."

Der Herr schaut ihm herüber: „Es ist mein Lieblingsroß,
Doch das verstehst du besser, so reit' es nur zum Troß."   50
Sie wechseln still, dann sprenget rasch, ohne Gruß und Wort,
Den Zügel lang verhänget, der edle Froben fort.

Und weit von seinem Herren hält er zu Rosse nun.
Für wenig Augenblicke scheint das Geschütz zu ruhn;
Der Kurfürst selber sinnet, warum es jetzt verstummt,   55
Und: „wacker war's gemeinet", der alte Dörfling brummt.

Da plötzlich donnert's wieder gewaltig über's Feld,
Doch nur nach einem Punkte ward das Geschütz gestellt;
Hoch auf der Schimmel setzet, Herr Froben sinkt zum Sand,
Und Roß und Reiter netzet mit seinem Blut das Land.   60

Die Ritter alle schauen gar ernst und treu darein.
O Froben dort am Boden, wie glänzt dein Ruhmesschein!
Der Kurfürst ruft nur leise:—„Ha! war das so gemeint?"
Und dann nach Feldherrnweise: „Nun vorwärts in den
     Feind!"

J. Minding.

28

„Prinz Eugen, der edle Ritter."

(1717)

Zelte, Posten, Werda-Rufer!
Lust'ge Nacht am Donauufer!
Pferde stehn im Kreis umher
Angebunden an den Pflöcken;
An den engen Sattelböcken   5
Hangen Karabiner schwer.

Um das Feuer auf der Erde,
Vor den Hufen seiner Pferde
Liegt das östreich'sche Piket.
Auf dem Mantel liegt ein Jeder,   10
Von den Tschako's weht die Feder,
Leutnant würfelt und Kornet.

Neben seinem müden Schecken
Ruht auf einer woll'nen Decken
Der Trompeter ganz allein: 15
„Laßt die Knöchel, laßt die Karten!
Kaiserliche Feldstandarten
Wird ein Reiterlied erfreun!

Vor acht Tagen die Affaire
Hab' ich, zu Nutz dem ganzen Heere,   20
In gehör'gen Reim gebracht,
Selber auch gesetzt die Noten:
Drum, ihr Weißen und ihr Rothen,
Merket auf und gebet Acht!"

Und er singt die neue Weise   25
Einmal, zweimal, dreimal leise
Denen Reitersleuten vor;
Und wie er zum letzten Male
Endet, bricht mit einem Male
Los der volle, kräft'ge Chor: 30

„Prinz Eugen, der eble Ritter!"
Hei, das klang wie Ungewitter
Weit in's Türkenlager hin.
Der Trompeter thät den Schnurrbart streichen
Und sich auf die Seite schleichen   35
Zu der Marketenderin.

                                        F. Freiligrath.

29

Prinz Eugenius, der edle Ritter.
(Volkslied)

Prinz Eugenius, der eble Ritter,
Wollt' dem Kaiser wied'rum kriegen

Stabt und Festung Belgarad.
Er ließ schlagen einen Brucken,
Daß man kunnt' hinüber rucken   5
Mit d'r Armee wohl für die Stabt.

Als der Brucken nun war geschlagen,
Daß man kunnt' mit Stuck und Wagen
Frei passir'n den Donaufluß:
Bei Semlin schlug man das Lager,   10
Alle Türken zu verjagen,
Ihn'n zum Spott und zum Verbruß.

Am einundzwanzigsten August so eben
Kam ein Spion bei Sturm und Regen,
Schwur's dem Prinzen und zeigt's ihm an,   15
Daß die Türken futragiren,
So viel als man kunnt' verspüren,
An die dreimalhunderttausend Mann.

Als Prinz Eugenius dies vernommen,
Ließ er gleich zusammenkommen   20
Seine General und Feldmarschall.
Er thät sie recht instrugiren,
Wie man sollt' die Truppen führen
Und den Feind recht greifen an.

Bei der Parole thät' er befehlen,   25
Daß man sollt' die Zwölfe zählen
Bei der Uhr um Mitternacht.
Da sollt' All's zu Pferd aufsitzen,
Mit dem Feinde zu scharmützen,
Was zum Streit nur hätte Kraft.   30

Alles saß auch gleich zu Pferde,
Jeder griff nach seinem Schwerte,

Ganz still rückt' man aus der Schanz.
Die Musketier wie auch die Reiter
Thäten alle tapfer streiten: 35
's war fürwahr ein schöner Tanz!

Ihr Constabler auf der Schanze,
Spielet auf zu diesem Tanze
Mit Karthaunen groß und klein,
Mit den großen, mit den kleinen—   40
Auf die Türken, auf die Heiden,
Daß sie laufen all' davon!

Prinz Eugenius wohl auf der Rechten
Thät' als wie ein Löwe fechten,
Als General und Feldmarschall.   45
Prinz Ludewig ritt auf und nieder;
„Halt't euch brav, ihr deutschen Brüder,
Greift den Feind nur herzhaft an!"

Prinz Ludewig, der mußt' aufgeben
Seinen Geist und junges Leben,   50
Ward getroffen von dem Blei.
Prinz Eugen war sehr betrübet,
Weil er ihn so sehr geliebet;
Ließ ihn bring'n nach Peterwardein.

30

Der Choral von Leuthen.

(5. December 1757)

Gesiegt hat Friedrichs kleine Schaar.   Rasch über Berg und
      Thal
Von dannen zog das Kaiserheer im Abendsonnenstrahl.

Die Preußen stehn auf Leuthens Feld, das heiß noch von der
     Schlacht,
Des Tages Schreckenswerke rings umschleiert mild die Nacht.

Doch dunkel ist's hier unten nur, am Himmel Licht an Licht,
Die goldnen Sterne ziehn herauf wie Sand am Meer so
     dicht,   6
Sie strahlen so besonders heut, so festlich hehr ihr Lauf,
Es ist, als wollten sagen sie: „Ihr Sieger, blicket auf!"

Und nicht umsonst. Der Preuße fühlt's: es war ein großer
     Tag.
Drum still im ganzen Lager ist's, nicht Jubel noch Gelag, 10
So still, so ernst die Krieger all', kein Lachen und kein
     Spott —
Auf einmal tönt es durch die Nacht: „Nun danket alle Gott!"

Der Alte, dem's mit Macht entquoll, singt's fort, doch nicht
     allein,
Kam'raden um ihn her im Kreis, gleich stimmen sie mit ein.
Die Nachbarn treten zu, es wächst lawinengleich der Chor, 15
Und voller, immer voller steigt der Lobgesang empor.

Aus allen Zelten strömt's, es reiht sich singend Schaar an
     Schaar,
Einfallen jetzt die Jäger, jetzt fällt ein auch der Husar.
Auch Musika will feiern nicht, zu reiner Harmonie
Lenkt Horn, Hobo' und Klarinett die heil'ge Melodie.   20

Und stärker noch und lauter noch, es schwillt der Strom zum
     Meer:
Am Ende, wie aus einem Mund, singt rings das ganze Heer.
Im Echo donnernd wiederhallt's das aufgeweckte Thal,
Wie hundert Orgeln braust hinan zum Himmel der Choral.

                                  H. Besser.

31

Der König und der Müller.

Es wohnt ein Müller sorgenfrei
In seiner kleinen Mühle.
Das Mühlchen klappert Brot herbei
Bei Sonnenbrand und Kühle.

Nicht weit davon ein König hatt'   5
Ein Schloß sich aufgebauet.
Wär' nicht die Mühl', man hätte Stadt
Und Land braus überschauet.

Der König bot dem Müller Geld:
„Verkauf' mir deine Hütte!   10
Bau neu sie auf, wo dir's gefällt,
Nach größerm Maß und Schnitte."—

„Mein Mühlchen ist mir gut genug,
Das laß' ich meinen Erben;
Es trägt des Vaters Segensspruch,   15
Hier will ich ruhig sterben."—

Der Fürst sagt ja, der Müller nein;
Der Fürst wird ungeduldig.
„Ich bin dein Herr; das Land ist mein;
Du bist zu weichen schuldig!"—   20

„Ich weiche nicht". — „Dann muß Gewalt
Den starren Sinn dir beugen."—
„Ihr irret, Herr, Euch werden bald
Die Richter andres zeigen."

„Die Richter?"—fällt dem König ein,   25
Die selbst er eingesetzet —

„Da haft du Recht; — ich geb' mich drein,
Dein Gut bleibt unverletzet!"

Seit jener Stunde lebten sie
Als Freunde, hoch und niedrig.   30
Des Schlosses Nam' ist Sanssouci,
Des Königs Name Friedrich.

Curtmann.

32
Der alte Ziethen.

Joachim Hans von Ziethen,
Husaren-General,
Dem Feind die Stirne bieten
Thät er die hundert Mal.
Sie haben's all' erfahren,   5
Wie er die Pelze wusch
Mit seinen Leibhusaren,
Der Ziethen aus dem Busch.

Hei, wie den Feind sie bläuten
Bei Lowositz und Prag,   10
Bei Liegnitz und bei Leuthen,
Und weiter, Schlag auf Schlag!
Bei Torgau, Tag der Ehre,
Ritt selbst der Fritz nach Haus,
Doch Ziethen sprach: „Ich kehre   15
Erst noch mein Schlachtfeld aus."

Sie kamen nie alleine,
Der Ziethen und der Fritz,
Der Donner war der eine,
Der andre war der Blitz.   20

Es wies sich Keiner träge,
Drum schlug's auch immer ein,
Ob warm', ob kalte Schläge,
Sie pflegten gut zu sein.

Der Friede war geschlossen;   25
Doch Krieges Lust und Qual
Die alten Schlachtgenossen
Durchlebten's noch einmal.
Wie Marschall Daun gezaudert,
Und Fritz und Ziethen nie,   30
Das ward jetzt durchgeplaudert
Bei Tisch in Sanssouci.

Einst mocht' es ihm nicht schmecken,
Und sieh, der Ziethen schlief.
Ein Höfling will ihn wecken,   35
Der König aber rief:
„Laßt schlafen mir den Alten!
Er hat in mancher Nacht
Für uns sich wach gehalten —
Der hat genug gewacht!"   40

Theodor Fontane.

33

Das Lied von Schill.

(1809)

Es zog aus Berlin ein tapferer Held,
Er führte sechshundert Reiter in's Feld,
Sechshundert Reiter mit redlichem Muth,
Sie bürsteten alle Franzosenblut.

Auch zogen mit Reitern und Rossen im Schritt   5
Wohl tausend der tapfersten Schützen mit;
Ihr Schützen, Gott segne euch jeglichen Schuß,
Durch welchen ein Franzmann erblassen muß!

So ziehet der tapfre, der muthige Schill,
Der mit den Franzosen schlagen sich will;   10
Ihn sendet kein Kaiser, kein König aus,
Ihn sendet die Freiheit, das Vaterland aus.

Bei Dobendorf färbten die Männer gut
Das fette Land mit französischem Blut;
Zweitausend zerhieben die Säbel blank,   15
Die übrigen machten die Beine lang.

Drauf stürmten sie Dömitz, das feste Haus,
Und jagten die Schelmenfranzosen hinaus;
Dann zogen sie lustig ins Pommerland ein,
Da soll kein Franzose sein Kiwi mehr schrei'n.   20

Auf Stralsund stürmte der reisige Zug;
O Franzosen, verstündet ihr Vogelflug!
O wüchsen euch Federn und Flügel geschwind!
Es nahet der Schill, und er reitet wie Wind.

Er reitet wie Wetter hinein in die Stadt,   25
Wo der Wallenstein weiland verlegen sich hat,
Wo der zwölfte Karolus im Thore schlief;
Jetzt liegen ihre Mauren und Thürme tief.

O weh euch Franzosen! wie mäht der Tod!
Wie färben die Reiter die Säbel roth!   30
Die Reiter sie fühlen das deutsche Blut,
Franzosen zu tödten, das däucht ihnen gut.

B.   6

O wehe dir, Schill! du tapferer Held!
Was sind dir für bübische Netze gestellt!
Viele ziehen zu Lande, es schleichet vom Meer   35
Der Däne, die tückische Schlange, daher.

O Schill! o Schill! du tapferer Held!
Was sprengst du nicht mit den Reitern ins Feld?
Was schließest in Mauern die Tapferkeit ein?
Bei Stralsund da sollst du begraben sein.   40

O Stralsund, du trauriges Stralesund!
In dir geht das tapferste Herz zu Grund',
Eine Kugel durchbohret das redlichste Herz,
Und Buben sie treiben mit Helden Scherz.

Da schreiet ein frecher Franzosenmund: 45
„Man soll ihn begraben wie einen Hund,
Wie einen Schelm, der auf Galgen und Rad
Schon fütterte Krähen und Raben satt."

So trugen sie ihn ohne Sang und Klang,
Ohne Pfeifengetön, ohne Trommelklang,   50
Ohne Kanonenmusik und Flintengruß,
Womit man Soldaten begraben muß.

Sie schnitten den Kopf von dem Rumpf ihm ab
Und legten den Leib in ein schlechtes Grab;
Da liegt er nun bis an den jüngsten Tag,   55
Wo Gott ihn in Freuden erwecken mag.

Da schläft nun der fromme, der tapfre Held,
Ihm ward kein Stein zum Gedächtniß gestellt;
Doch hat er gleich keinen Ehrenstein,
Sein Name wird nimmer vergessen sein.   60

Denn sattelt ein Reiter sein schnelles Pferd,
Und schwinget ein Reiter sein blankes Schwert,
So rufet er zornig: Herr Schill! Herr Schill!
Ich an den Franzosen euch rächen will.

E. M. Arndt.

34

Hofers Tod.

(20. Februar 1810)

Zu Mantua in Banden
Der treue Hofer war,
In Mantua zum Tode
Führt ihn der Feinde Schaar;
Es blutete der Brüder Herz,   5
Ganz Deutschland, ach! in Schmach und Schmerz,
Mit ihm das Land Tyrol.

Die Hände auf dem Rücken
Der Sandwirth Hofer ging,
Mit ruhig festen Schritten,   10
Ihm schien der Tod gering,
Der Tod, den er so manches Mal
Vom Iselberg geschickt in's Thal,
Im heil'gen Land Tyrol.

Doch als aus Kerkergittern   15
Im festen Mantua
Die treuen Waffenbrüder
Die Händ' er strecken sah,
Da rief er laut: „Gott sei mit euch,
Mit dem verrathnen deutschen Reich   20
Und mit dem Land Tyrol!"

6—2

Dem Tambour will der Wirbel
Nicht unterm Schlägel vor,
Als nun der Sandwirth Hofer
Schritt durch das finstre Thor.   25
Der Sandwirth noch in Banden frei,
Dort stand er fest auf der Bastei,
Der Mann vom Land Tyrol.

Dort soll er niederknieen,
Er sprach: „Das thu’ ich nit!   30
Will sterben, wie ich stehe,
Will sterben, wie ich stritt,
So wie ich steh’ auf dieser Schanz’:
Es leb’ mein guter Kaiser Franz,
Mit ihm sein Land Tyrol!“   35

Und von der Hand die Binde
Nimmt ihm der Korporal,
Und Sandwirth Hofer betet
Allhier zum letztenmal;
Dann ruft er: „Nun, so trefft mich recht!   40
Gebt Feuer! — Ach, wie schießt ihr schlecht!
Ade, mein Land Tyrol!“

Julius Mosen.

35
Der Trompeter an der Katzbach.
(1813)

Von Wunden ganz bedecket,
Der Trompeter sterbend ruht,
An der Katzbach hingestrecket,
Der Brust entquillt das Blut.

Brennt auch die Todeswunde,   5
Doch sterben kann er nicht,
Bis neue Siegeskunde
Zu seinen Ohren bricht.

Und wie er schmerzlich ringet
In Todesängsten bang,   10
Zu ihm herüberbringet
Ein wohlbekannter Klang.

Das hebt ihn von der Erde,
Er streckt sich starr und wild.
Dort sitzt er auf dem Pferde   15
Als wie ein steinern Bild.

Und die Trompete schmettert —
Fest hält sie seine Hand —
Und wie ein Donner wettert
Victoria in das Land.   20

Victoria — so klang es,
Victoria — überall
Victoria — so drang es
Hervor im kräft'gen Schall.

Doch als es ausgeklungen,   25
Setzt die Trompet' er ab,
Das Herz ist ihm zersprungen,
Vom Roß stürzt er herab.

Um ihn herum im Kreise
Hielt's ganze Regiment.   30
Der Feldmarschall sprach leise:
„Das heißt ein selig End!"

Julius Mosen.

36

Das Lied vom Feldmarschall.

(1813)

Was blasen die Trompeten? Husaren, heraus!
Es reitet der Feldmarschall im fliegenden Saus;
Er reitet so freudig sein muthiges Pferd,
Er schwinget so schneidig sein blitzendes Schwert.

O schauet, wie ihm leuchten die Augen so klar!　　　5
O schauet, wie ihm wallet sein schneeweißes Haar!
So frisch blüht sein Alter wie greisender Wein,
Drum kann er Verwalter des Schlachtfeldes sein.

Der Mann ist er gewesen, als alles versank,
Der muthig auf gen Himmel den Degen noch schwang; 10
Da schwur er beim Eisen gar zornig und hart,
Den Wälschen zu weisen die deutsche Art.

Den Schwur hat er gehalten. Als Kriegsruf erklang,
Hei! wie der weiße Jüngling in'n Sattel sich schwang!
Da ist er's gewesen, der Kehraus gemacht,　　　15
Mit eisernem Besen das Land rein gemacht.

Bei Lützen auf der Aue, da hielt er solchen Strauß,
Daß vielen tausend Wälschen der Athem gieng aus,
Viel Tausende liefen dort hasigen Lauf,
Zehntausend entschliefen, die nimmer wachen auf.　20

Am Wasser der Katzbach er's auch hat bewährt,
Da hat er den Franzosen das Schwimmen gelehrt:
Fahrt wohl, ihr Franzosen, zur Ostsee hinab!
Und nehmt, Ohnehosen, den Wallfisch zum Grab!

Bei Wartburg an der Elbe wie fuhr er hinburch!   25
Da schirmte die Franzosen nicht Schanze noch Burg,
Da mußten sie springen wie Hasen über's Feld
Und hell ließ erklingen sein Hussa! der Held.

Bei Leipzig auf dem Plane, o herrliche Schlacht!
Da brach er den Franzosen das Glück und die Macht,   30
Da liegen sie so sicher nach blutigem Fall,
Da ward der Herr Blücher ein Feldmarschall.

Drum blaset, ihr Trompeten! Husaren, heraus!
Du reite, Herr Feldmarschall, wie Winde im Saus!
Dem Siege entgegen zum Rhein, über'n Rhein,   35
Du tapferer Degen, in Frankreich hinein!

E. M. Arndt.

37

Lützow's wilde Jagd.

(1813)

Was glänzt dort vom Walde im Sonnenschein?
   Hör's näher und näher brausen.
Es zieht sich herunter in düsteren Reih'n,
Und gellende Hörner schallen darein,
   Und erfüllen die Seele mit Grausen.   5
Und wenn ihr die schwarzen Gesellen fragt:
Das ist Lützow's wilde verwegene Jagd.

Was zieht dort rasch durch den finstern Wald
   Und streift von Bergen zu Bergen?
Es legt sich in nächtlichen Hinterhalt;   10
Das Hurrah jauchzt und die Büchse knallt,

Es fallen die fränkischen Schergen.
Und wenn ihr die schwarzen Jäger fragt:
Das ist Lützow's wilde verwegene Jagd.

Wo die Reben dort glühen, dort braus't der Rhein,   15
   Der Wüthrich geborgen sich meinte,
Da naht es schnell mit Gewitterschein
Und wirft sich mit rüst'gen Armen hinein,
   Und springt an's Ufer der Feinde.
Und wenn ihr die schwarzen Schwimmer fragt: 20
Das ist Lützow's wilde verwegene Jagd.

Was braus't dort im Thale die laute Schlacht?
   Was schlagen die Schwerter zusammen?
Wildherzige Reiter schlagen die Schlacht,
Und der Funke der Freiheit ist glühend erwacht   25
   Und lodert in blutigen Flammen.
Und wenn ihr die schwarzen Reiter fragt:
Das ist Lützow's wilde verwegene Jagd.

Was scheidet dort röchelnd vom Sonnenlicht,
   Unter winselnde Feinde gebettet?   30
Es zuckt der Tod auf dem Angesicht,
Doch die wackeren Herzen erzittern nicht;
   Das Vaterland ist ja gerettet!
Und wenn ihr die schwarzen Gefallnen fragt:
Das war Lützow's wilde verwegene Jagd.   35

Die wilde Jagd und die deutsche Jagd
   Auf Henkersblut und Tyrannen!
Drum, die ihr uns liebt, nicht geweint und geklagt!
Das Land ist ja frei und der Morgen tagt,
   Wenn wir's auch nur sterbend gewannen!   40

Und von Enkeln zu Enkeln sei's nachgesagt:
Das war Lützow's wilde verwegene Jagd.

Theodor Körner.

38
Auf Scharnhorst's Tod.
(28. Juni 1813)

In dem wilden Kriegestanze
Brach die schönste Heldenlanze,
Preußen, euer General.
Lustig auf dem Feld bei Lützen
Sah er Freiheitswaffen blitzen,   5
Doch ihn traf der Todesstrahl.

„Kugel! raffst mich doch nicht nieder?
Dien' euch blutend, werthe Brüder,
Führt in Eile mich gen Prag!
Will mit Blut um Oestreich werben;   10
Ist's beschlossen, will ich sterben,
Wo Schwerin im Blute lag."

Arge Stadt! wo Helden kranken,
Heil'ge von den Brücken sanken,
Reißest alle Blüthen ab;   15
Nennen dich mit leisen Schauern —
Heil'ge Stadt! nach deinen Mauern
Zieht uns manches theure Grab.

Aus dem irdischen Getümmel
Haben Engel in den Himmel   20
Seine Seele sanft geführt,
Zu dem alten deutschen Rathe,
Den im ritterlichen Staate
Ewig Kaiser Karl regiert.

„Grüß' euch Gott, ihr theuern Helden!   25
Kann euch frohe Zeitung melden:
Unser Volk ist aufgewacht!
Deutschland hat sein Recht gefunden!
Schaut! ich trage Sühnungswunden
Aus der heil'gen Opferschlacht!"   30

Solches hat er dort verkündet,
Und wir Alle stehn verbündet,
  Daß dies Wort nicht Lüge sei.
Heer, aus seinem Geist geboren,
Jäger, die sein Muth erkoren,   35
  Wählet ihn zum Feldgeschrei!

Zu den höchsten Bergesforsten,
Wo die freien Adler horsten,
  Hat sich früh sein Blick gewandt;
Nur dem Höchsten galt sein Streben,   40
Nur in Freiheit konnt' er leben,
  Scharnhorst ist er drum genannt.

Keiner war wohl treuer, reiner;
Näher stand dem König Keiner, —
  Doch dem Volke schlug sein Herz.   45
Ewig auf den Lippen schweben
Wird er, wird im Volke leben,
  Besser als in Stein und Erz.

. Max von Schenkentorf.

39

Blücher am Rhein.

(1813)

Die Heere blieben am Rheine stehn:
Soll man hinein nach Frankreich gehn?
Man dachte hin und wieder nach,
Allein der alte Blücher sprach:
„Generalkarte her!   5
Nach Frankreich gehn ist nicht so schwer.
Wo steht der Feind?" — „Der Feind? — Dahier!"
„Den Finger drauf, den schlagen wir!
Wo liegt Paris?" — „Paris? — Dahier!"
„Den Finger drauf! das nehmen wir!   10
Nun schlagt die Brücken über'n Rhein;
Ich denke, der Champagnerwein
Wird, wo er wächst, am besten sein!"

Kopisch.

40

Die Wacht am Rhein.

Es braust ein Ruf wie Donnerhall,
Wie Schwertgeklirr und Wogenprall:
Zum Rhein, zum Rhein, zum deutschen Rhein!
Wer will des Stromes Hüter sein?
Lieb' Vaterland, magst ruhig sein,   5
Fest steht und treu die Wacht am Rhein.

Durch Hunderttausend zuckt es schnell,
Und Aller Augen blitzen hell:

Der deutsche Jüngling, fromm und stark,
Beschirmt die heil'ge Landesmark.
Lieb' Vaterland, magst ruhig sein,
Fest steht und treu die Wacht am Rhein.

Auf blickt er in des Himmels Blau'n,
Wo todte Helden niederschau'n,
Und schwört mit stolzer Kampfeslust:
Du, Rhein, bleibst deutsch wie meine Brust!
Lieb' Vaterland, magst ruhig sein,
Fest steht und treu die Wacht am Rhein.

Und ob mein Herz im Tode bricht,
Wirst du doch drum ein Wälscher nicht.
Reich, wie an Wasser deine Flut,
Ist Deutschland ja an Heldenblut.
Lieb' Vaterland, magst ruhig sein,
Fest steht und treu die Wacht am Rhein.

So lang ein Tropfen Blut noch glüht,
Noch eine Faust den Degen zieht,
Und noch ein Arm die Büchse spannt,
Betritt kein Feind hier deinen Strand!
Lieb' Vaterland, magst ruhig sein,
Fest steht und treu die Wacht am Rhein.

Der Schwur erschallt, die Woge rinnt,
Die Fahnen flattern hoch im Wind:
Zum Rhein, zum Rhein, zum deutschen Rhein!
Wir Alle wollen Hüter sein!
Lieb' Vaterland, magst ruhig sein,
Fest steht und treu die Wacht am Rhein.

Max Schneckenburger.

41

Die Schlacht vor Metz.

(14., 16. und 18. August 1870)

Das war eine Schlacht!
Drei Tage lang
Vom Morgen bis zur sinkenden Nacht
Der männermordende Donner kracht'
Und des Todes mähende Sichel klang.   5

Das war eine Schlacht!
Zwischen Kampf und Kampf
Hat der Tod je einen Rasttag gemacht,
Umnebelt vom schwebenden Pulverdampf,
Satt und übersatt   10
Des Blutes, das er zu gierig trank,
Vom blutigen Mähen so müd' und matt,
Daß dem knöchernen Arm die Sichel entsank.

Das war eine Schlacht!
Und als des dritten Tages Gestirn   15
Zur Rüste ging und von der Berge Firn'
Ihren Schattenschleier senkte die Nacht,
Da lagen, Freund und Feind,
An die Dreißigtausend vereint,
Im stummen Tode friedlich gesellt —   20
Ein unabsehbar Leichenfeld.
Und auf das klaffende Völkergrab
Lächelt der Mond vom Sternenzelt
Schweigend des Todes Frieden herab.

Das war eine Schlacht!   25
Die ihr, das Vaterland

Zu schützen vor Gewaltthat und Schand',
Euch selber zum blutigen Opfer gebracht —
Ihr treuen Todten, du und du,
Die im Gefecht   30
Mit dem Leben besiegelt Deutschlands Recht,
Niedergemäht von des Todes Maht,
Ausgesät als des Friedens Saat,
Fahrt wohl, zur ewigen Ruh'!

Das war eine Schlacht!   35
Des Feindes Plan, so keck erdacht,
Zu Schanden gemacht,
Zerrissen, zerschlissen wie sein Heer!
Er selbst, nach knirschender Gegenwehr
Zurückgeworfen in die Feste Metz!   40
Dort fest umsponnen mit ehernem Netz,
Mit eiserner Klammer regungslos
An den Fels geschmiedet bewegungslos,
Aller Hülf' und alles Entrinnens baar,
Aufbäumend in ohnmächtigem Schmerz —   45
Und der deutsche Aar
Stückweis ihm zerhackend das zuckende Herz!
Das war eine Schlacht!
Westwärts in wehender Fahnen Pracht,
Mit klingendem Spiele dran und drauf,   50
In nimmer aufgehaltenem Lauf
Weit, weit übern Rhein
Nach Frankreich hinein
Deutschlands Banner tragend, sein Recht und Ehr',
Im Sturmmarschtritt,   55
Im Siegesschritt,
Wälzt gen Paris sich das deutsche Heer.

                                                   Dohm.

42

Kaiser von Deutschland! Dich grüsst mein Lied.

(18. Januar 1871)

Kaiser von Deutschland! Dich grüßt mein Lied
   Mit Orgelschall und Glockenklange,
Und Alles, was in Lüften zieht,
   Stimmt brausend ein zu dem Gesange!
Von unsern Bergen donnert's nieder,   5
   Mit unsern Wogen rauscht's empor,
Von Strand zu Strande hallt es wieder,
   Von Fels zu Fels ein Jubelchor.

Der alte Rothbart ist erwacht
   Und schwingt sein Schwert vom Bergesgipfel, 10
Still ward die Rabenbrut der Nacht,
   Und Adler jauchzen um die Wipfel:
„Verjüngt ist uns das Reich erstanden,
   Am Kaiserthrone kniet der Sieg.
Aus blut'ger Saat in Feindeslanden   15
   Empor der Einheit Eiche stieg!"

Rings fliegt durch die bekränzten Gau'n
   Der Freude ahnungssel'ges Leben,
Mit trunknen Jünglingsaugen schaun
   Hinaus wir in ein neues Leben;   20
Es leuchtet uns in goldnem Glanze
   Ein Volkesfrühling wunderreich,
Auch in der Reiche vollem Kranze
   Nicht eines prangt dem unsern gleich.

Ihr Kämpfer aus dem heil'gen Streit,   25
  Ihr Freiheitssänger hochgemuthet,
Du Jugend treu und todbereit,
  Die du gelitten und geblutet,
Erfüllt sind eures Lebens Träume,
  Bald wird der Bau vollendet sein,   30
Nun führt in seine hohen Räume
  Der Kaiser alle Brüder ein.

Du Held warst Führer uns zur Macht,
  Du wirst es nun zur Freiheit werden,
Gibst frei den Geist, verscheuchst die Nacht,   35
  Verwaltest gleiches Recht auf Erden!
O Dir fliegt jedes Herz entgegen,
  Es streckt nach Dir sich jede Hand:
O schütte stets uns reichern Segen
  Auf's theure deutsche Vaterland!   40

                                        K Elze.

NOTES.

I.

THE Visigoths (𝔚eſtgothen) had been conducted into Italy by their brave and politic king Alaric; in the year 410 they had sacked Rome and carried off immense booty. Gibbon, who relates this at great length in his *History of the Decline and Fall of the Roman Empire*, chap. XXXI., gives the following account of the event which forms the subject of Platen's ballad: "The whole design [of crossing to Sicily] was defeated by the premature death of Alaric, which fixed, after a short illness, the fatal term of his conquests. The ferocious character of the Barbarians was displayed in the funeral of a hero, whose valour and fortune they celebrated with mournful applause. By the labour of a captive multitude they forcibly diverted the course of the *Busentinus*, a small river that washes the walls of *Consentia*. The royal sepulchre, adorned with the splendid spoils and trophies of Rome, was constructed in the vacant bed; the waters were then restored to their natural channel, and the secret spot, where the remains of Alaric had been deposited, was for ever concealed by the inhuman massacre of the prisoners who had been employed to execute the work."

We subjoin also the account found in the *Historia Miscella* (p. .313, 11 ss. ed. Eyssenh.): *Gothi Basentium amnem de alveo suo captivorum labore derivantes, Alaricum in medio eius alveo cum multis opibus sepeliunt amnemque meatui proprio reddentes, nequis locum scire possit, captivos qui interfuerant extinguunt.*

1. The shades of the Goths are here represented as wandering ever up and down, near the spot where their king was buried. 𝔇umpf (muffled) and liſpeln (to mutter, lisp) refer to the spectral singing, which is reechoed by the waters of the river.

2. 𝔚irbel, the eddies of the river.—Observe the indefinite subject es. We are left to imagine that the king's own shade sends up the answer.

B.   7

4. In prose: ten beſten Mann, ter iṣrem Volfe je turch ten Tob entriſſen worten war.

5. The more usual construction is fern von ter Ṣeimat.

6. Jugentlocfen = jugentliche Locfen.—In prose we should employ the plural Schultern.

7. Observe that the poet has changed the original account, according to which captives were employed to do the work.—um tie Wette = wetteifernt, 'vying with one another.'

9. wogenleer, free from water (after the river had been turned into another channel).—Ṣöṣlung denotes the deep bed of the river.

11. feine ſtolje Ṣabe, the proud trophies buried with Alaric.

12. Stromgewächfe, river-plants, e.g. rushes and reeds.—wüchfen, subj. preter. of wachfen (ich wuchs).

14. fchäumen, to rush foaming into, etc.

15. There is emphasis in the expression Männer, which involves the notion of 'stout men and true.'

16. tir, dativus ethicus, commonly left untranslated in English.— verfchren = verleṣen, verunehren.

17. Observe the omission of the perſonal pronoun fie, which is, however, peculiar to poetry and a higher style of composition.

II.

Chlodewig or, as he is commonly called, *Clovis* conquered the greater part of Gaul (his victory over Syagrius, the Roman ruler, was obtained A.D. 486), and established the rule of the Franks over that country; he then beat the Alemanni, a Germanic tribe that dwelt on either side of the Rhine, from its sources to its conflux with the Maine and the Moselle. Gibbon relates, "Clovis encountered the invaders of Gaul [the Alemanni] in the plain of Tolbiac [Zülpich] about twenty-four miles from Cologne [this is, however, a controverted statement]; and the two fiercest nations of Germany were mutually animated by the memory of past exploits and the prospect of future greatness. The Franks, after an obstinate struggle, gave way, and the Alemanni, raising a shout of victory, impetuously pressed their retreat. But the battle was restored by the valour, the conduct, and perhaps by the piety of Clovis, and the event of the bloody day decided for ever the alternative of empire or servitude. In the distress of the battle of Tolbiac, Clovis loudly invoked the God of Clotilda [his queen] and the Christians; and victory disposed him to hear with respectful gratitude the eloquent

Remigius, bishop of Rheims, who forcibly displayed the temporal and spiritual advantages of his conversion. The king declared himself satisfied of the truth of the Catholic faith. The important ceremony was performed in the cathedral of Rheims." (Chap. XXXVIII.)

1. In prose we say exclusively, die Schlacht von or bei Zülpich.

3. More commonly as a compound, das Kampfgedränge, the throng of battle.

4. Troß, 'train,' especially of menials. See also note on Kohlrausch, p. 77, 3.

7. mein Gemahl is poetical and archaic instead of meine Gemahlin. Luther often says Gemahl instead of Gemahlin, e.g. St Matth. i. 20, 24, Joseph, fürchte dich nicht, Mariam, dein Gemahl, zu dir zu nehmen, and in his smaller Catechism, daß...ein Jeglicher sein Gemahl liebe und ehre. [Here Gemahl denotes both husband and wife.] In Old High German the current forms are *gemahela* and *gemalu*. Clotilda possessed such influence over her husband that he had allowed his two sons to be baptized even before his own conversion.

8. So = wenn; in the same manner *so* is used in Early English.

11. so, 'then'; if that condition be fulfilled.

12. After the verb lehren we often find the infinitive without zu.

13. Sprach es = kaum hatte er es gesprochen, als. Comp. *dixit et* in Virgil, and ἦ ῥα καί in Homer.

16. siegesmuthig, confident of victory.

17. We say both der Schreck and der Schrecken. The plural is die Schrecken and Schrecknisse (from das Schrecknis).—It is more common to employ the reflective form sich wenden of fleeing enemies (*terga vertunt*).

19. zugleich, i.e. with him.

20. vor, like the Latin *prae*, above.

III.

Gelimer, the last king of the Vandals in Africa, had long held out, in the mountain fastness of Papua, in the inland country of Numidia, against Pharas, an officer employed by Belisarius. See the account of Gibbon, chap. XLI.

5. *Maurusii* is in Latin less common than *Mauri*, the aboriginal Numidians. The Greeks say Μαυρούσιοι.

6. In prose: weder Brod noch Wein.

11. der Griechen Heer, the army sent by Justinian, the 'Roman' Emperor at Constantinople. The Greek Emperors retained the name

of 'Roman' ('Ρωμαῖοι) to the very last, and hence the Greeks of the middle ages styled themselves 'Ρωμαῖοι.

13. er is the Vandal king; in the next line, er denotes of course the enemy.

17. ber Hüter des Heeres is an unusual expression; in prose we should .say, ber Führer or Anführer des Heers.

. 18. "From the Vandal messenger, Pharas was informed of the motives of this singular request." Gibbon.—The sense of the line is: ' Did not Gelimer add his motives for this strange request?'

21—32 contain the explanation given by the messenger.

24. The first foot of this line (Jn bie Berg-) is an anapæst.

25. han is the archaic form of the infinitive instead of haben, of which it is originally a contraction.

26. fein is the gen. of the personal pronoun, just as in er gebenfet fein, 'he remembers him.' Comp. the Greek τοὺς ὀφθαλμοὺς αὐτοῦ. .In prose we should employ the possessive, feine Augen. Comp. 5, 13, 50.

28. Als, but, except.

31. barein = accompanying (the music). Comp. Unb gellenbe Hörner ſchallen barein. Körner, *Lützow's wilde Jagd* (37, 4).

IV.

The Merovingian kings in Gaul soon sank to the disgraceful position of mere puppets—*rois fainéants*, as the French call them—and the actual power of rule fell into the hands of their *Majores domus*. Pepin of Landen became the founder of a family of *Majores domus*, who succeeded in uniting all the royal prerogatives in their hands long before the royal title was assumed by them. *Pepin II.* of Heristall († 714) was recognised as *dux et princeps omnium Francorum*; his son, *Charles Martel*, obtained a splendid victory over the Saracens at Tours, in 732, and left at his death (A. D. 741) his power to his two sons *Pepin*, surnamed the Short, on account of his small stature, and *Karlmann*, who died A. D. 747, thus leaving the whole to Pepin. In 751 Pope *Zacharias* (comp. v. 13 in the present poem) pronounced Pepin to be lawfully entitled to the royal name and dignity, and in 752 the nobility of the Franks, congregated at Soissons, deposed the last Merovingian, and proclaimed Pepin king of the Franks. The ballad given by us recounts a feat of prowess performed by Pepin.

3. Jn aller Weise = in jeder Beziehung, (in) every way.

4. Volksberather, lit. counsellor of the nation.

6. We say personally, er ist mir (meinen Augen) ein Wohlgefallen, *deliciae meae.* The more common use of the word appears, however, in such a sentence as this: das wird mir zu besonderem Wohlgefallen gereichen, 'this will afford me special gratification.'

7. nur sich selber gleich, i.e. there was nobody to be compared with him.

8. vor Allen, *praecellens omnibus.*

11. des Hammers Sohn: Pepin's father, Charles, was surnamed *Martel,* i.e. 'hammer.'

12. erkoren (from er-küren, of which word there is another form, kiesen, akin to Engl. *choose* and Fr. *choisir*) is a more dignified expression than gewählt. Comp. the noun Kurfürst, elector.

15. der Hort, protector, orig. refuge. In the Bible, the Lord is often styled ein starker Hort, and der Hort des Heils. Comp. an instance below, 17, 101. Originally a neuter, this word became masculine in Middle High German. It is identical in origin with the E. *hoard,* and even Goethe employs it in this sense, e.g. ihr kennt den weiten wohlver-wahrten Hort (quoted in Grimm, *wörterb.* IV. 2, 1835).

16. alle Welt might remind us of the Fr. *tout le monde* = everybody; but we should rather understand the expression in its original sense: the whole world, *orbis terrarum.* Comp. also below, v. 89.

18. It might also be manchen.

19. Die is the demonstrative pronoun; if it were the relative, the verb would stand at the end of the sentence.

20. meistern is an invidious term = mäkeln or aussetzen; it always denotes unmerited reprehension.

21. Deß = darob or darüber.

22. dämpfen is often used metaphorically in the sense of allaying or suppressing. Goethe, e.g., has a predilection for it in this sense: see Grimm, *wörterb.* 2, 718.

23. There are the two forms er läßt and er labet. Comp. Schiller, *Tell* (beginning): es lächelt der See, er ladet zum Bade.—männiglich, a somewhat antiquated adverb, corresponding to the Lat. *viritim.*

25. mit Drang = in a throng, im Ge-dränge.

27. Die Trommete (also Drommete) is less usual than die Trompete.

29. We do not say ein gedankenschwerer Mann, but ein gedankenschweres Antlitz. The compound adj. gedankenvoll is more common, the opposite is denoted by gedankenleer and gedankenlos.

30. Ungewitter (n.), storm, tempest. There is but a very slight differ-ence of meaning between Gewitter and Ungewitter. The prefix ge- inten-sifies the original Wetter, and un- adds the notion of bad, unfavourable. Wetter in itself is often used to denote a tempest.

31. Blitze denotes here the rapid glances of the eye; so also blitzende Augen, 'quick-glancing eyes.' Comp. v. 42.

33. Leu, a poetical form instead of Löwe.

38. Ur (i.e. Urochs, Auerochs) = Stier, 33. So again v. 65.—Ge-nicke (n.), of the same root as *neck*, G. Nacken (m.).

39. der Plan, 'level surface,' is often used of a smooth arena.

44. In prose: daß er die Beute dem Löwen entreißt, or die Beute......zu entreißen.

45. große Augen machen denotes 'to stare' (lit. make large eyes, open his eyes very wide).

48. In German, it is not necessary to add an infinitive of a verb of motion after a modal verb like wollen, können, mögen, müssen. We may therefore say, er will nach England, he wishes *to go* to England. In the Elizabethan period, the English language possessed the same facility of construction, comp. e. g. Shaksp. *Coriol.* II. 3, 157, *will you along*, i.e. will you *go* along, and see Abbott, *Shaksp. Gramm.* § 405.

49. wie = während.

52. der Strauß, plur. Sträuße, is a somewhat poetical word instead of Streit or Kampf. This is a different word from der Strauß, a nosegay.

57. der Graus (Middle High G. *der grûs*) is derived from grauen, 'to be afraid of' (es graut mir vor etwas), whence also the adj. grausig and grausenhaft, 'terrible.' The verb is grausen, which is commonly imper-sonal, e.g. der Brunnen war so tief, daß mir grausete, hinein zu sehen, though it occurs also as a personal verb in the *Appendix to Luther's Bible*, 4 Ezra v. 14, mein Leib grauste sehr und meine Seele ängstigte sich, *my body was sorely afraid and my soul was harassed.* The infinitive of this verb is used as a substantive in the next line.

59. The expression is short and pregnant. In prose we should say, er zieht sein Schwert...heraus. It is also more common to say, aus der Scheide heraus.

68. die Schranke, the barrier; the plural more commonly used in the sense required here; die Schranken, the lists. So below, v. 86.

75. A better, though less common form is sprützen. Comp. also Schiller, *Taucher*: Bis zum Himmel sprützet der dampfende Gischt.

77. Der Recke is an old word, now used only in a higher style of writing, instead of der gewaltige, starke Mann.

79. Kampfrevier = Kampfbezirk. This word is omitted in Grimm's *Dictionary*. Revier (n.) is a word derived from Ital. *riviera*, Fr. *rivière*, in the general sense of 'district.' It is very common in modern German and belongs, moreover, to the earliest importations from the Romance languages.

81. die Spötter werth = die werthen (i. e. edlen) Spötter. In poetry, the adj. is frequently placed after the subst.

82. This is an absolute construction of the participle, corresponding to a Latin abl. abs. *oculis deiectis*. The same construction would be permitted in French, *les yeux baissés*. A very good instance of this absolute construction occurs in Schiller's ballad, die Bürgschaft:

> Da sinkt er an's Ufer und weint und fleht,
> Die Hände zum Zeus erhoben,

i. e. *manibus ad Iovem sublatis*. The noun is in the accusative, comp. 27, 52, and Aue § 373.

87. It was the ancient custom of the Franks and of the German tribes generally to proclaim their king by lifting him up on their shields.

91. Observe the omission of the auxiliary hat in the relative sentence. It is not a very common phrase, einen Löwen fällen, in the sense of tödten, niederschlagen, überwinden, the Latin *caedere*. It should be borne in mind that, just as from *cadere* is formed *caedere*, we have in German fallen and fällen, in English *to fall* and *to fell*.

92. Demüthiglich is an instance of adverbial formation by means of the suffix lich, which corresponds to the Engl. *-ly*.

93. der Barde (originally a Celtic word) denotes an inspired minstrel; the word has become part and parcel of our poetic phraseology since the time of Klopstock (second half of the 18th century).

V.

Charlemagne (*Karl der Grosse*), the son of Pepin, reigned from 768—814 (at first together with his brother Karlmann who died 771); in 800 he was crowned Emperor by Pope Leo III. In the legends of the middle ages, Charlemagne forms the central figure of a group of heroes (Palatine), among whom *Roland* is the most conspicuous. According to tradition, Roland was nephew to Charlemagne, being the son of his (merely legendary) sister Bertha and Count Milon of Anglante (i.e. Angers); but the genuine records of history know no more of Roland than that he was marquis of Brittany, in which quality he occurs in Eginhard. This writer relates (c. ix.) that Eghart, Anshelm, and Rutland (i.e. Roland) fell at Roncevalles during the retreat from Spain, which country had been invaded by Charles in 778. Uhland has written a series of ballads on the legends of Roland, and one of them, containing a marvellous act of valour performed by the boy Roland, has been selected by us. The subject-matter appears to be entirely of Uhland's own invention.

2. The city of Aachen (*Aix-la-Chapelle*) was Charlemagne's favourite place of residence. He was also buried there in the splendid Cathedral founded by himself.

3. das Wildpret, venison. This is the common form, though Wild-bret or Wildbrät would be a better spelling, the second part of the word being derived from braten (Wild zum Braten). In Middle High German the word is *daz wiltbræte.*

6. Observe the omission of the copula und between the two adjectives. This would be inadmissible in prose.

9. der Schimmer = Schein, v. 5.

13. See note on 3, 26, and below, v. 50.

14. der Ardennerwald, *les Ardennes.* It is also usual to say die Ardennen; comp. v. 30.

18. feiern, to delay, = müßig sein. Compare the sentence quoted from Niebuhr by Grimm, *wörterb.* 3, 1437: So lag das römische Heer müßig, der Krieg feierte. See below 11, 3.

19. Stahlgewand, lit. 'steel dress,' i.e. armour. Gewand (from old Germ. wât = Engl. *weed,* in *widow's weeds*) denotes any kind of habit. Observe the perfect sie haben begehrt, instead of the more correct sie begehrten, which would, moreover, be in closer agreement with the next line. The employment of the perfect as a narrative tense (perf. hist.) is in German limited to the popular style and dialects.

20. heißen, with the infinitive without zu, corresponds to the Greek κελεύειν, Engl. *to bid.*

23. More correctly it would be lieber Vater. The shorter form is often used by children.

24. This is a shortened conditional clause, instead of wenn ihr mich auch zu schwach vermeint (i.e. wähnet, glaubt) or mich für zu schwach haltet.

26. winzig, tiny.

28. Samt (not much used in prose as a preposition) is of the same root as the well-known zu-samm-en; this sam being identical with the English *same* and the Greek ἅμα. Comp. v. 172 and v. 189, where we have zusammt.

32. Da thäten sie sich trennen is said in imitation of the tone of the popular ballads, instead of the correct ba trennten sie sich. See below, v. 60.

33. In prose: hinter seinem Vater.

37. In prose: umherstreifen.—Degen (originally derived from *dîhen*= (ge)teihen ('to thrive') in modern German, and akin to Greek τέκνον, Old Saxon *thegan*, whence the well-known *thane*, all these words originally denoting 'boy' or 'son') is often used in poetic diction in the sense of *hero*. In the ancient poem of the Nibelunge Hagen is often styled *der küene degene*.

39. das Ge-heg, wood; an intensified form of der Hag, v. 152. (Comp. *the Hague*, the capital of the Netherlands.)—The omission of weder before noch is poetical.

41. More correctly it ought to be schlafend; he lay sleeping, or asleep. But the form preferred by Uhland is, perhaps, more conformable to the popular tone observed throughout this ballad. It is, however, quite correct to say, sich schlafen legen.

47. es, i.e. das Blitzen und Leuchten.

50. er gedachte is more emphatic than the simple verb.

51. Schrecken = Schreckniß, object of terror.

53. The expression would be completed as follows: während er noch im besten Schlafe ist.

58. Das Waffen is archaic instead of die Waffe. Comp. v. 165.

60. See note on v. 32.

62. ganz sachte, quite softly.—der Tann is archaic instead of der Tannenwald. Comp. below, v. 173.

66. Der Fant, 'a wight' (so again v. 206), from Ital. *fante* which is abbreviated from *infante*=Lat. *infans*. In Dutch *vent* means a young fellow or lad, and even in Old High German we find *fendo*, 'a foot-soldier,' comp. *infantry*.

68. It might also be so lang wie er. It is, perhaps, more correct to use als after a comparative, and wie after a positive.

69. schier, almost, nearly—an old word (M.H.G. *schiere*).

73. die Tartsche, 'a shield,' is in this form derived from the old Fr. *la targe*, but originally the word is Anglosaxon *targe*, corresponding to High Germ. die Zarge, the border of a buckler.

79. auslangen, to reach forward, as far as possible.

88. unbehende, not agile enough, unwieldy: behende is from O. G. *be hende*, 'by (the) hand, at hand.' Compare the phrase bei der Hand sein, 'to be at hand, ready,' and hence 'to be quick, alert.'

89. schlug = traf.

95. mit Schmerzen, with a sad (sorrowing) heart.

101. We more commonly use the compound ein Blutstrom.

104. licht = leuchtend (scheinend, glänzent, strahlent).

106. gut should be taken as an adverb.

107. We say both ter Quell and tie Quelle.

110. In prose it is zurück. The trisyllabic form employed by Uhland is, however, the original one.—jung, instead of junge. Comp. vv. 22 and 23.

112. schlafent should be understood as accusative: *invenit eum dormientem.*

114. In English we say *overcome with,* or *conquered by sleep.* (The Greek idiom is quite parallel to the German, ὕπνῳ δαμείς.)

121. We have now had three feminine substantives of the same formation: tie Ferne, tie Weite, tie Wilte. Thus we also say tie Nähe. The subst. used in the present line is not so common as the others. See also v. 205.

122. Comp. v. 33.

125. hätt', instead of hatte, is in the tone of popular poetry.—jüngst, 'a short while ago.'

127. It is common to say, er kann kaum seinen Augen glauben (or trauen). Comp. also the proverb, was meine Augen sehen, glaubt mein Herz.

130. So = welches or tas. This use of fo, instead of the relative pronoun, is very antiquated. Observe also the omission of the auxiliary hatte.

133. In prose we should be obliged to add the article, ter Rumpf.

137. In prose war would be placed at the end of the sentence.

139. Etwas verschlafen means to lose by sleeping, to sleep away.

141. stunt is a less common form of the imperf. than stant.

143. gesunt was formerly used in a wider sense than now; here it means not only 'healthy,' but whole and unhurt.

144. weilen, to tarry.

148. Muth is commonly used in modern German in the sense of 'courage'; it is, however, originally the same as the Engl. *mood,* which may, perhaps, be employed here to translate it (e.g. 'with moody brow').

152. Comp. v. 39.

156. It might also be tes Riesen Hantschuh. The compound expresses a wider idea than the original genitival term, ein Riesenhantschuh being a glove fit for a giant, and the other meaning one actually belonging to a giant.

157. ungefüg, uncouth.

158. aus = heraus or hervor.

159. schön instead of schönes.—Reliquienstück, a somewhat jocular expression, 'a specimen of a relic.' Comp. Waffenstück, v. 174.

165. See note on v. 58.—The form lange is now only used as an adverb of time, and produces a very peculiar and quaint effect in the present passage.

167. Bavarian beer is considered the best of the various kinds brewed in Germany.—Schluck, draught.

171. die Wehr(e): comp. our note on Kohlrausch, p. 26, 1.

175. The omission of es before the verb is in conformity with popular speech.

176. ferne = von ferne, or in der Ferne, at a distance.

178. Der = dieser.—deß = dessen, gen. of possession: *huius est.*

181. 'I should very much like to have.'

184. lenkte, viz. sein Pferd.

191. Observe the difference between the German and the English idioms: sie kamen geritten (gegangen, gefahren, gelaufen, etc.), they came *riding.* Comp. 7, 1; 13, 2.

193. in der Mitten is archaic instead of Mitte.

195. wunderklar, wondrously clear.

199. frohgemuth instead of mit frohem Muthe, this being the opposite of the expression read v. 148. A more common word is wohlgemuth, 'cheerful' (8, 2).

204. gewandt, instead of the compound umgewandt (or umgedreht in vulgar parlance).

205. die Helle: see note on v. 121.

207. Geselle is often used like *lad* or *fellow.* Originally the word means one who shares a room with somebody else, ge + sal = Saal, 'hall.' Comp. the parallel expression *comrade,* from *camera,* 'room.'

208. Um Gott, 'for God's sake'; comp. *perdy* in old French and English.

209. Wicht, the same word in point of etymology and of meaning as *wight,* is now commonly used as a contemptuous term.

210. Derweil = the while (though the German is orig. a genitive of die Weile), is obsolete as a conjunction. Comp. 19, 41.—eben, just. In English we should say, 'while you happened to be asleep.'

VI.

Wittekind (or *Wittikind*) was the valiant leader of the Saxons, against whom Charlemagne waged fierce and bloody wars. In his first war, A.D. 772, he destroyed the Irminsul, the foremost sanctuary of these pagan tribes, and founded many Christian chapels throughout the country. In the second war, A.D. 778—780, Wittekind obtained a victory on the Süntel mountains, but was subsequently beaten at Verden and in other battles. He submitted to Charlemagne in 785, and was then baptized. The present poem relates a legend connected with Wittekind's conversion.

2. Der morgenrothe Schein = ter Glanz der Morgenröthe (dawn).

5. In prose: mit leifen Schritten. For leife, leife comp. 12, 19.

9. It is not common to say, einen Streit fechten; the usual phrases are einen Kampf führen, einen Streit austämpfen. But we also say quite commonly einen Streit ausfechten.

11. fonter is more poetical than ohne.

12. 'The Lord of Christendom' is Charlemagne, who was then the most powerful prince of the Christian world.

15. Helbenfelle denotes the furs in which the German warriors were then still dressed and which marked them at once as such (Helten). This compound is omitted in Grimm's *Dictionary.*

16. Is there not a contradiction between feig here and kühn, v. 13? There is not: but we leave the student to unravel this difficulty for himself.

17. umrungen, by poetical licence for umringt, 'surrounded.'

24. ganze = einzige, sole.

26. erglühen is here used of the rising of the sun.

27. innig schwoll: Charlemagne's heart expanded in love and piety.

32. Die Glorie is often used of splendour, magnificence.

34. golbturchwirkt, embroidered in gold.

35. Maged is the old form of the modern word Magd, which is applied by the mediæval writers to the Virgin Mary, 'the pure maiden.'

41. brünstig (derived from brenn-en, 'to burn'), is often used of ardent zeal and piety.—ftillanbächtig, in silent prayer.

43. Charlemagne delegated the administration of the several provinces of his states to Counts, *comites,* Grafen (O. H. G. *grâveo, grâvo,* mediæval Latin *graphio,* A.S. *geréfa,* Engl. *reeve.* Comp. Marfgraf, Burggraf, Landgraf, etc. with *sheriff* (=shire-reeve), *borough-reeve, town-reeve,* etc.

47. The plural bie Angeſichter is not so common as tie Geſichter.

49. tie Päre, or Pairs, the peers.

51. himmliſch, i.e. with heavenly food.

53. teß = tatob or beßhalb. We generally say ob einer Sache ſtaunen.

54. bem Gotte, according to Wittekind's pagan conception.

57. The old Christian name was ἀγάπαι, literally translated by Liebesmahl.

61 sqq. The poet alludes to the doctrine of transubstantiation. The miracle consists in the fact of this process becoming visible to Wittekind, while it remains hidden from the communicants. In the original edition of this poem by Platen, a different miracle stands in the place of this transubstantiation scene.

65. erlachen (not a common word), 'break into smiles.'

68. ſelig (from *sala*, 'fortune') means originally 'happy.' We may say 'blessed,' as this does not exclude the idea of terrestrial bliss. Our word 'silly' is the same as the Germ. ſelig, having successively meant (1) blessed, (2) innocent, (3) harmless, (4) weakly, foolish. See Trench, *Select Glossary*.

70. empfahen is poetical and archaic instead of empfangen.

72. bas Zugegenſein is a somewhat awkward expression, denoting 'presence,' Gegenwart.

75. ſpaltet = zertheilt, dissevers.

76. heibniſch is the adverb.

VII.

Louis the Pious (called *le débonnaire* by the French), the son and successor of Charlemagne, reigned from 814—840. The latter part of his reign and life was disturbed and made wretched by the renewed rebellions of his unnatural sons, Lothar, Pepin, Louis, and Charles. When, in 838, Louis (surnamed the German) had raised his arms against his father, the old Emperor's heart broke, and full of sorrow and misery he concluded his life in an island in the river Rhine, not far from Ingelheim.

1. For the construction see n. on 5, 191.

6. In prose: weich gebettet.

10. bie Au(e) is here used in its original sense of an island surrounded by water on all sides. In M.H.G. *ouwe* means 'water' = O.H.G. *aha* = Lat. *aqua*. The more usual sense of this word in modern

German is 'a well-watered district.' The word is, however, now almost confined to the poetical style or an elevated composition.

12. The plural bie Lüfte is exclusively used in the sense of 'breezes.'

21 sq. The construction des Rheines Welle rauscht mir ein sanftes Schlummerlied is poetical, instead of das Rauschen der Wellen des Rheins klingt mir wie ein sanftes Schlummerlied.

24. Observe the position of the adjectives after the noun.

26. 'His word was fulfilled' means 'his request was carried out.'

28. Inselport, an unusual word probably not registered in many dictionaries, 'the landing-place of the island.' A safe place of anchoring is called Port in the elevated style, and Hafenbucht or Bucht in familiar language. Comp. the lines quoted by Sanders, *Deutsche Synonymen*, p. 137:

> Mit leichtem Muthe knüpft der arme Fischer
> Den kleinen Nachen an im sichern Port,
> Sieht er im Sturm das große Meerschiff stranken.

The island in which Louis died ('*in quadam insula contigua Magontiacae civitati*' is the expression of a contemporary historian) is now called Petersau. Louis possessed a villa in this secluded spot.

35. Of the palace of Charlemagne at Ingelheim a contemporary poet employs the expression '*alta domus centum perfixa columnis.*' There are no remains left now of this building.

36. The palaces of the Emperors were often styled Saal; comp. der Saalhof at Frankfort-on-the-Maine, erected by the Emperor Lewis the Pious, when Charles the Bald was born.

38. Meine Stunde schlägt = 'my hour is come.'

44. The suffix ling denotes 'sonship.' Hence Karolinger, the descendants of Karl (Charlemagne). The last Carlovingian who united once more the whole Empire of Charlemagne, was Louis's grandson, Charles the Stout (Karl der Dicke), who was, however, deposed by the German vassals at Tribur in 887; the last Carlovingian who reigned in Germany was Louis the Child (Ludwig das Kind), who died A. D. 911. In France, the Carlovingian dynasty maintained itself on the throne until the year 987, when Hugo Capet was elected king.

46. Observe the expressive alliteration in this line.

48. vatermild, 'mild (kind), like a father.'

54. Umglänzt is formed like umstrahlt, 'surrounded with a lustre.'— flüchtig, 'transitory.'

55. Lothar was Emperor until 855. The country of Lothringen (Lorraine) still bears his name.

57. Scepter is generally used as a neuter in accordance with the gender it bears in Greek and Latin (σκῆπτρον, *sceptrum*), but we find it also as a masc.: der Scepter. Comp. e.g. the following passage in Jung-Stilling's *Life* (p. 470, ed. Reclam): Alle diese Verklärten führen dich dann vor den Thron des Allerbarmers, er neigt den Scepter aller Welten gegen deine Stirne. And it may be observed that foreign words are apt to change their gender in German, e.g. das Labyrinth = ὁ λαβύρινθος, der Punct = punctum, der Altar = altare (n.), der Pact = pactum, etc., or French *la rencontre* as compared with Germ. das Rencontre.

60. gnügt instead of genügt.

61. Twice before the Emperor Louis had been compelled to abdicate by his rebellious sons.

67. den Kampf bestehen, 'to pass honourably through a struggle.'

72. Comp. v. 47.

VIII.

After the decease of the last Carlovingian (911), *Conrad of Franconia* was elected king of Germany. He reigned until 918. On his deathbed he is said to have directed the vassals to carry the crown to his most powerful adversary, Henry, Duke of Saxony, surnamed *der Finkler* or *Vogler*, 'the Fowler.' The (legendary) reason of this surname is related in the present poem: Henry, being very fond of the sport of netting birds, is said to have been engaged in it when messengers came to apprise him of his having been elected king. Carlyle calls him 'the grand old Henry' in his *Frederick the Great*, b. II. ch. I.

2. wohlgemuth: see n. on 5, 199.

3. Perlen denotes the pearly dew-drops.

8. The song of the nightingale is usually connected with the evening, although it does sing during the day.

11. Was gilt's? literally, 'what is it worth?' Hence, 'what do you give for it?' Used in betting, 'what are the odds?' here as an exclamation.—'nen = einen.

12. lugen, 'to spy,' akin to E. *look*.—Himmelszelt is a poetical term denoting the 'sky' as a tent stretched above the earth; comp. v. 34.

15 sq. The construction is was für eine Reiterschaar sprengt denn dort herauf?—denn is expressive of surprise and, to some extent, of indignation.

19. Daß Gott, an elliptic phrase, to be completed by such words as es ihnen vergelte.

21. ꜩꜩ Ꜩroꝭ : see n. on 2, 4.
26. The complete construction is (𝔚ir ſuchen) unſern 𝔥errn.
28. 𝔖tern is often used to denote preeminence and excellence.
30. They do homage by kneeling down silently.
32. In prose: 𝔈ꜩ iꝭ deꝭ teutſchen 𝔯eicheꝭ 𝔚ille.
36. wie 𝔇ir'ꝭ gefüllt, (be it) as thou pleasest.

IX.

Henry I. reigned from 919—936. He was a wise and energetic prince, who founded many towns and obtained a splendid victory over the wild Hungarian hordes at Merseburg, 933. Henry's son, Otho I. or the Great (936—973), surpassed even his father in energy and power. He endeavoured to break the power of the vassal dukes whose influence had become too great for their sovereign. Eberhard, the duke of Franconia, felt offended by a fine imposed on him, and contrived to seduce Otho's brothers, Thankmar and Henry, to rebel against the king. Thankmar was killed in this rebellion, and Henry was forced to submit in 939; but the pardon granted to him by the generous Otho could not render him faithful to his brother. He conspired again with the Archbishop of Mayence and some dissatisfied nobles to stab the king at Quedlinburg, about Easter, 940. The conspiracy was, however, discovered, and the Archbishop and Henry were imprisoned. Then it was that repentance awoke in the heart of the misguided youth; he escaped from the prison, which he could not endure, and in penitential garb he threw himself at his brother's feet in the Cathedral Church at Frankfort-on-the-Maine, and obtained pardon and reconciliation, for which he prayed fervently. The concord and agreement of the brothers remained undisturbed ever after. It will be seen that there is a slight inaccuracy in the present ballad, in which the scene of the reconciliation is laid at Quedlinburg, instead of Frankfort. There is another error in the title given to Otho. Previous to the year 962, in which he was crowned Roman Emperor, Otho bore no other title but that of King, 𝔎önig.

3. 𝔐acht is used here in the sense of military force; translate ' with the puissant array of his knights.'

4. The common form is 𝔚eihnacht. Comp. v. 48.

6. Comp. 4, 31.

10. In prose we should more commonly say, er hat die Feinde (acc.) abgewehrt.

13. For the plural Lande see our note on Goethe's *Hermann and Dorothea*, 1, 204.

14. This phrase is very common with the negation: das will mir nicht in den Sinn, I cannot get myself to believe this.

16. was = weshalb, warum.

18. The Roman Catholic Church considers the consecration of the host as a renewed sacrifice of the Lord.—die Messe, the mass, Lat. *missa*, said to be derived from the old form of dismissing the congregation, 'Ite, missa est' (sc. congregatio). Messe also means 'a fair.'

20. brünstig, see n. on 6, 40.

22. Das Hemde is the old form, while in modern German das Hemb is more usual.

24. ihm is dativus ethicus; in English this should be translated as if it were seine Kniee.

25. der Fehl is poetical instead of der Fehler, though always with a more emphatic meaning, = Verbrechen or Vergehen. This word is repeatedly used by Luther in his translation of the Bible. Comp. St Matth. vi. 15: so ihr den Menschen ihre Fehle nicht vergebet, so wird euch euer Vater eure Fehle auch nicht vergeben.

26. The construction is, hier liege ich dir zu Füßen.—In prose we should either say um Verzeihung flehen or Verzeihung er flehen.

30. Otho had pardoned his brother, granting him his life after the conspiracy, and merely sentencing him to imprisonment. By his escape from prison Henry had forfeited his life and pardon.

35. The expression is proverbial. To denote absolute stillness we also say man hätte eine Nadel zu Boden fallen hören können, 'you might have heard a pin drop to the ground.'—Laub = *leaf*, commonly Blatt. In modern German Laub is commonly used as a collective.

41 sqq. The passage referred to in the following verses runs as follows in Luther's translation:—Da trat Petrus zu ihm und sprach: Herr, wie oft muß ich denn meinem Bruder, der an mir sündiget, vergeben? Ist es genug siebenmal? Jesus sprach zu ihm: Ich sage dir, nicht siebenmal, sondern siebenzigmal siebenmal. St Matth. xviii. 21 and 22. .

45. The tears are called unbewußt, 'unconscious,' as they start into the Emperor's eye without his knowing it.

B. S

X.

Otho the Great was succeeded by his son Otho II. who reigned until 983. His wife was a Greek princess, Theophano, by whom he had a son, Otho III., a highly talented youth, but unfortunately destitute of resolution and energy. Otho III., whose whole mind was bent upon the revival of the splendour of the imperial titles, reigned until 1002, and sank into an early grave, worn out with the struggles and toils of his reign. In the year 999, he had ordered the tomb of Charlemagne at *Aachen* to be opened, and had descended into it in order to revive his flagging enthusiasm by the sight of the dead Emperor, whose majestic appearance is said to have produced an overwhelming impression on the mind of the phantastic youth.

3. Otho III. died in the castle of Paterno, near mount Soracte, not far from Rome. He had not yet completed his twenty-second year.

7. Lenz (comp. *lent*) is poetical instead of Frühling; comp. our note on Schiller's *Maid of Orleans*, Prol. 2, 14.

15. Rome is built upon seven hills.

16. In Danish and Swedish *hav* (*haf*) means the sea in general, but in the north of Germany this name has been restricted to three large bays of the Baltic—or rather three lakes close to the Baltic; though connected with the sea by a channel, they contain sweet water and are separated from the ocean by a long narrow strip of sandhills (Nehrung): 1. das Kurische Haff at the mouth of the Niemen; 2. das frische Haff at the mouth of the Nogat, an arm of the Vistula; 3. das Pommersche or Stettiner Haff at the mouth of the Oder: all three on the coast of Prussia.

17. Das Seelenreich = Tottenreich, 9, 34.

18. Harren is construed with the genitive, after the analogy of warten. See Aue § 349.

21. Crescentius, a Roman patrician, had broken his faith to Otho III., expelled Gregory V. whom Otho had placed on the papal see, and put John (who had formerly been Otho's tutor in Greek) in his place. When Otho took Rome in 998, John was terribly mutilated and blinded by the exasperated German warriors, while Crescentius was beheaded in the Castel San Angelo, in which he had defended himself. Gregory died in the year after these atrocities, 999, and his death was ascribed by the people to divine vengeance for his cruelty towards the unfortunate John.

27. Otho II. died when his son was about three years old.

30. The strong formation of the imperf. of fragen is less usual in modern German than the weak. In the works of the classical writers, frug occurs in not a few passages.

31. The poet himself has the note: Otto II. liegt bekanntlich in ter Peterskirche begraben.

33. Comp. the expression Volksberather, 4, 4.

35. Aeltervater = Urgroßvater, Henry I.

39. Mathilde was the queen of Henry I.

44. The logical order of words would be schon als Kind.

46. Atóm = ἄτομον, the small particles out of which, according to some philosophers, the world is composed.

47. eine nichtige Sache, *res nihili.*

52. Der kaiserliche Staub means the dead body of the young Emperor.

58. Das Panier is derived from the Fr. *la bannière*, which has also passed into the German language in the shape of das Banner.

60. Kaiserzier = kaiserliche Pracht, imperial splendour.

64. barg, instead of verbarg, in the sense of verhüllte or bedeckte.

66 sq. Otho's dead body was escorted across the Alps by his faithful Germans through the opposing hosts of the hostile Italians; it was then deposited in its final resting place at *Aachen.*

71. thatenlos, 'void of deeds'; thatenreich, 'rich in deeds' (comp. 1 Tim. vi. 18).

XI.

" The Church of Rome has raised Henry II. to a place among her Saints, and legendary tales describe this king as a monk in purple, a crowned penitent, scarcely able to drag along his weary flesh. But History shows a different portrait of King Henry. It attests that he was one of the most active and energetic rulers that ever sat on the German throne; it teaches us to recognise his acute mind and a great talent for organisation, such as was rarely seen in those days." Giesebrecht, *History of the German Emperors*, II. 95 sq. The same writer relates the subject of the present poem in the following manner :— " In 1008 there appeared a strange vision to the king, as the legend goes. He fancied that he was in the monastery of St Emmeran at Regensburg, praying at the tomb of his former teacher, Wolfgang; this one—he thought—came up to him and pointed to some writing on the wall close by. There the king saw the mysterious words, 'After six.' He thought that he was destined to die after six days, and therefore devoted himself entirely to works of charity and piety. The six days passed by without anything befalling him, and there likewise passed six months and six years. But on the seventh anniversary of the vision, Henry was crowned Emperor at Rome, Febr. 14, 1014." (Giesebrecht, l. c. II. 118, cf. 614.)

3. Wo=wann. The adverbs of place are often used of time.— Brüter=Ortensbrüter, i.e. monks.—feiern, 'to cease' from work, or here, from praying. Feiern is derived from the mediæval Latin, *feriare=ferias agere.* Comp. n. on 5, 18.

8. Sanct Heimeran=St Emmeran, *vide suprà.* The ancient monastery of St Emmeran was founded as early as 652, but the present edifice is a collection of buildings of various later epochs. It belongs now to the princely house of Thurn and Taxis, and forms their general residence.

12. umnachtet=umgeben von Nacht.

13. gar=vollends.

17. es schien=ein Schein fiel über ihn. Observe the impersonal construction of the verb.

19. that er blicken: comp. 13, 26.

20. ein heil'ges Angesicht instead of das Angesicht eines Heiligen.

22. ein lichter Bischof, the figure of a bishop all illumined with rays of light.

26. The expression is very peculiar, though it may be readily understood. The whole figure of the bishop seemed to consist of light and radiance, hence also his fingers shine like tapers upon the writing.

28. It is common German to say, mit ten Augen or mit tem Blicke auf etwas treffen.

30. We say commonly, Einem etwas auf's Wort glauben. The present phrase may be considered as an imitation of this.

32. schwanb = verschwanb.

36. Lebenshell should rather be joined with Morgenroth than with Wangen, though even this is not altogether impossible.

37. gekommen, sc. ist.

40. Lebensfrist, lease of life.

42. Mond may be taken both as *moon* and *month.* Comp. n. on 16, 29.

43. We should join stets würtiger, always increasing in worthiness.

47. sonter is more poetical than ohne.

50. Leuchtenb is evidently used in allusion to v. 26. Henry himself had increased in sanctity, and was at the same time radiant with earthly splendour.

52. The omission of the definite article before Röm'ſche Königskrone is very unusual and tends to impart to this passage a certain flavour of archaic dignity.

54. Observe the preposition von instead of the genitive. We may also say, Herr über alles deutſche Land.

55. dort instead of damals. See n. on v. 3.

59. treulich is an adverb, from treu. Adverbs are often formed with the suffix lich. Comp. n. on 4, 92.

XII.

Weinsberg, a small town in the modern kingdom of Würtemberg, not far from Heilbronn, is famous for the event celebrated in the present ballad. The ruins of the ancient stronghold of the *Weibertreu* may still be seen on a rock overhanging the town, and in one of the churches of the place there is a small picture (painted 1659) of the women carrying their husbands and brothers away on their backs. In the wars between Conrad III. (1138—1152), the first king of the celebrated Hohenstaufen dynasty, and Heinrich the Proud, Weinsberg was besieged by Conrad's troops, and it was then that the event celebrated in this ballad is said to have taken place. The adherents of the Hohenstaufen party were called *Waiblinger*, which the Italians turned into *Ghibellini;* their adversaries were styled *Welfen*, in Italian *Guelfi.* (Waiblingen was one of the seats of the Hohenstaufen family.) Conrad is very properly styled 'king' in the present poem, as he never went to Rome to be crowned. The titles Emperor and King are, however, very often confounded.

3. Neſt = the home of a family or community, especially when situated on a height (comp. Num. xxiv. 21, and Horace *Od.* III. 4, 14). It is now often applied contemptuously to a small town.

4. feſthalten = behaupten.

5. The German proverb is der Hunger iſt ein ſcharfer Dorn.

7. Degen, 'brave man'; see n. on 5, 37.

8. This is a shortened conditional clause = und wenn ihr auch die Thore öffnet.

9. kommen is an old form of the past participle repeatedly used by Luther in his translation of the Bible, instead of gekommen.

10. vom Blute rein, in as far as they have not shared in the fighting.

11. den Armen, the poor women. The expression denotes commiseration.—Der Held is Conrad.

13. Etwas frei haben, to be free to take something. Comp. the phrase employed in the German railway service: ein Reisender hat fünfzig Pfund Gepäck frei, a passenger is allowed fifty pounds of luggage (carriage-free).

17. Der Morgen graut is a common expression, even in prose, of the first dawning of day.

18. vom Lager (her): the spectators look from the camp towards the town.

19. das bedrängte Thor = das Thor der bedrängten (belagerten) Statt.—leise, leise means 'very softly'; comp. also 6, 5. Repeating the adjective is a frequent mode of intensifying the idea of it, comp. also the familiar *bon-bon.*

22. Der Eheherr (commonly used in the trisyllabic form) is a more formal and respectful appellation than Ehemann or the simple Mann.

23. arg = arglistig, cunning.—Wicht, 'wight,' a fellow of the train.

24. bedeutsam, with a tone full of meaning. In this sense Goethe uses the participle bedeutend (*Hermann and Dorothea,* 4, 111).

25. der fromme Herr is Conrad. He is styled fromm here because he keeps his promise even under the construction laid upon it by these cunning women.

27. In English we may say, 'what has been said, cannot be unsaid.'

28. zerdeuteln is a very unusual word. The suffix -eln expressing pettiness, deuteln means to attempt to change the sense of a word by petty and paltry shifts; the prefix zer- denotes division and dissipation. The meaning of the whole expression would therefore be, 'to get rid of a royal pledge by means of a petty interpretation.'

29. Gold der Krone should be understood of the splendour of the regal dignity and faith.

30. herüber, to us; hinüber, to others.

XIII.

Frederick I., or *Barbarossa* (i.e. 'Red-beard'), the most glorious Emperor of the Hohenstaufen dynasty, reigned from 1152—1190. At the close of his reign, he took the Cross and went on a crusade into the Holy Land, the kings of France (Philip Augustus) and of England (Richard Cœur de Lion) being engaged in the same enterprise. Frederick perished while bathing in the river Calycadnus in Syria.

The present ballad narrates, in a quaint and popular style, an episode of this Crusade. It is based upon a passage in the Byzantine historian, Nicetas Acominatos of Chonae, who relates it in his second book, in the *Life of the Emperor Isaac Angelus*, previous to the battle of Iconium (May 18, 1190). Before Uhland, this tale had been further embellished by J. P. Abelin and the famous preacher Abraham a Santa Clara, who was the first to state that the valiant German knight was a Swabian. (See Götzinger, *Deutsche Dichter*, I. p. 519.) There is a dash of local patriotism in it, the poet Uhland being himself a Swabian. It should be observed that Schwabenstreich commonly means a mad and reckless prank. The Swabians are likewise said not to grow rational before the fortieth year of their age.

1. lobesam is a somewhat antiquated and quaint word, of pretty much the same meaning as vortrefflich, ehrenwerth. Comp. einsam, beredsam, etc.

2. For the construction er kam gezogen, see n. on 5, 191.

3. Das fromme Heer, the army of the Crusaders. They are called 'pious' on account of the religious nature of their expedition.

5. The imperf. erhub is less usual in modern German than erhob. Both forms are derived from the old imperfect *erhuob*.

8. The Germans have always had a certain reputation for hard drinking. In that sterile and dry district many a German knight had to forego his favourite pastime owing to the scarcity of drink.—Sich (dat.) etwas abthun means the same as sich etwas abgewöhnen.

10. die Mähre originally means 'the horse' in general, but in modern German it is often used in the contemptuous sense of a jaded horse.

15 sq. Er würde es nie aufgegeben haben, auch wenn es ihn das eigene Leben gekostet hätte.—nimmer is a stronger negation than nie. The word is, moreover, very frequently used in the Swabian dialect in the place of the simple negation.

19. in die Quer(e), across the road.

20. Both funfzig and fünfzig are in use.

23. Er forcht sich nit is purposely put in the Swabian dialect, instead of the correct er fürchtete sich nicht.

24. Schritt vor Schritt, 'step by step.' We may also employ the preposition für in this phrase.

25. spicken is properly used of the 'larding' of joints.

26. See n. on 5, 60.

27. Die Zeit wird mir zu lang, I find the time too long for me.

28. Perhaps the compound Krummſäbel (omitted in Grimm's *Dictionary*) is more commonly used of the Turkish *scimitar*.

29. See our note on Goethe's *Hermann and Dorothea*, 4, 153.

34. mit Macht, ' with all his might ' or ' amain.'

37. The usual phrase is in Stücke hauen.

41. For the noun der Graus, see n. on 4, 57.

42. in alle Welt hinaus is a proverbial phrase, like ' everywhere and anywhere.'

43. Es ist mir, als wenn (ob)... I feel, as if...

45. In the phrase des Weges kommen (ziehen, wandern, reiten, &c.) we should observe the idiomatic use of the genitive. Compare Homer, *Iliad*, B. 801 ἔρχονται πεδίοιο, Τ. 285 ἐπειγόμενός περ ὁδοῖο, &c.

47. mit gutem Bedacht = the adv. bedächtig, ' at their good leisure.'

48. In prose we should say was für Arbeit. In the phrase employed by Uhland, Arbeit should be understood as a genitive = *quid laboris*.

52. It should be observed that der Streich means (1) the stroke, the blow, (2) the trick, the feat.

53. The Swabians are witty, and never at a loss for an answer and retort, in spite of their proverbial slowness.

54. im Schwange ſein or gehen, ' to be in fashion,' a very idiomatic phrase. Comp. e.g. Luther's translation of Psalm lxxxv. 14, daß Gerechtigkeit dennoch vor ihm bleibe und im Schwange gehe. 2 Maccab. iii. 1, als man nun wieder in gutem Friede zu Jerusalem wohnete und das Geſetz ſein im Schwange ging.

56. halt is a kind of asseverative interjection much used in the Swabian dialect. It may, perhaps, be rendered by the Irish *faith*.

XIV.

Under the Emperor Frederick I. the German Empire attained its greatest splendour and power, and that heroic Emperor succeeded in making himself feared and respected both at home and abroad. It is for this reason that the German people have long cherished his memory, and conceived an idea that the Emperor was not dead, but merely sleeping and biding his time in the *Kyffhäuser*, in Thuringia. Jacob Grimm, in his *German Mythology*, p. 906 sq., gives the following account of this legend, which may serve as a kind of commentary upon Rückert's ballad:

Auf dem Kyffhäuser in Thüringen ſchläft Friedrich Rothbart: er ſitzt am runden Steintiſch, den Kopf in der Hand haltend, nickend, mit den Augen zwinkernd, sein Bart wächst um den Tisch und hat schon zweimal dessen Rundung umschlossen; wann er das drittemal herum gewachsen sein wird, erfolgt des Königs Aufwachen. Bei seinem Hervorkommen wird er seinen Schild hängen an einen dürren Baum, davon wird der Baum grünen und eine bessere Zeit werden. Doch Einige haben ihn auch wachend gesehen; einen Schäfer, der ein ihm wohlgefälliges Lied gepfiffen, fragte Friedrich: „Fliegen die Raben noch um den Berg?", und als der Schäfer bejahte: „So muß ich hundert Jahre länger schlafen." (See also Grimm's *Deutsche Mythologie*, p. 366.) It should, however, be stated that when the legend first appears it is related, not of Frederick I., but of his grandson, the Emperor Frederick II. It may be added that the Welsh similarly believe their ancient king Arthur to lie in Snowdon, and one of these days they expect him to come forth from the mountain and to reestablish the splendour of the kingdom of the *Cymry* by driving the *Saxons* out of Britain.

2. Friederich (i.e. rich in peace) is the original trisyllabic form of the name now commonly used as Friedrich.

12. zu seiner Zeit, 'in his own good time.'

14. Darauf as a relative is obsolete now; we should now say worauf, as we have it v. 16.

15. marmelsteinern is archaic, instead of marmorn, or aus Marmor.

17. His beard is not of flaxen colour, but as red as fire.

20. Observe the somewhat heavy accentuation ausrüßt, instead of the ordinary ausrüßt.

23. je denotes repetition after pauses, each of which is long.

24. Knabe and Knappe ('a page') were originally identical in meaning, and merely different forms of one and the same word. We may translate it here with the old English *knave*, which retained its original sense of 'page' in the language of Shakespeare.

XV.

The present ballad may be looked upon as an attempt to substantiate, by free and original invention, a title handed down from remote ages. The Counts of Limpurg (a castle situated at a short distance from Schwäbisch-Hall, in the modern kingdom of Würtemberg) claimed from times immemorial the title and privileges of cup-bearers to the German Emperor, and are repeatedly styled *pincernae de Limpurg* in ancient documents. They became extinct in 1713. As the tale related here is of Uhland's own invention, it remains uncertain which of the Hohenstaufen Emperors is the one spoken of in the present poem.

1. Die Feste (often spelt Voste) = Festung, stronghold.

5. allerwegen (properly two words of genitival formation) = überall.

8. leid is etymologically connected with E. *loth ;* hence Einem etwas verleiden may well be translated, 'to make some one loth to do something.'

11. Wilde Feder is apparently meant to denote the feather of a wild bird.

13. an der Seiten is purposely archaic instead of an der Seite; comp. Auc § 137, note. See also below, v. 75.

14. Buchs = Buchsbaumholz, boxwood.

15. schreiten = *incedere,* or like the compound ausschreiten.

17. For the plural Mannen see Aue § 148, note 2.—Instead of wohl ('indeed'), we might also turn the sentence this way: Obwohl (obschon, wenngleich) er Knechte und Mannen und ein tüchtiges Roß hatte, ging er, &c.

20. Troß, his menial train.

21. Geleite, company.

22. Comp. 5, 165.

26. The phrase adopted here is somewhat homely when used of Imperial state. But the poet employed it intentionally.

27. mit hellen Haufen, with a large and noisy train. Haufe is rather an undignified word: see n. on Kohlrausch, p. 1, 3.

29. vorrennen here = ansprengen, galloppiren.

31. Jagdgesinde means the same as Troß, v. 20. Gesinde is a collective noun derived from O. H. G. *sind,* corresponding to Gothic *sinþs* and Anglo-S. *sîð* 'road,' 'journey,' whence O. H. G. *kisindo,* Gothic *gasinþa* 'a roadfellow,' 'an escort.'

32. Forst always denotes an extensive forest, while Wald is the ordinary wood.

36. In prose: mit mannigfaltigen Blumen, *variis floribus.*

39. Die Häge, plural (rarely used) of der Hag, for which word see note on 5, 39.

40. A more usual order of words would be und vor ihm stand der Graf.

41. anheben is more dignified than anfangen, the original notion being that of *raising* his voice.

42. hie is archaic instead of hier. It is more frequently used in the compound allhie.

44. Both kommt and kömmt are correct forms of the third person sing. In the same manner we have both du kommst and du kömmst, but

in the first pers. sing., and in the whole plural the vowel cannot be modified.

45. ſtreifen: comp. 5, 37.

46. fahen is obsolete, instead of fangen. Comp. 6, 70.

49. ohn' alle Fährbe, without any evil thought or suspicion. The expression is not common. Grimm, 3, 1247, quotes another instance of it from Goethe:

> Darum ſchwör' ich feierlich
> Unb ohn' alle Fährte,
> Daß ich mich nicht freventlich
> Wegbegeben werbe.

55. pfänden = als ein Pfand ergreifen.

57. mir verfangen = von mir mit Beſchlag belegt. The expression is legal.

58. In poetry begehren is sometimes construed with a genitive, like verlangen; comp. the genitive used after ἐπιθυμῶ.

61. Das Gewälbe is an intensified derivation from ber Walb; comp. bas Gehege from ber Hag (5, 39).

62. mir, dat. ethicus, 'in my opinion,' or it may be ' to my loss.'

63. In prose: bei Hof unb im Felbe.

69. Ich habe etwas eigen, I possess something as my own, I own something.

72. 'mal instead of einmal; its use here is somewhat idiomatic. The sense of this line would require a different expression in prose, e.g. wenn ich erſt alt unb frank geworben bin.

74. Here mir is 'for me.'

78. thu' mir bas is a familiar and somewhat off-hand phrase, instead of thu' mir ben Gefallen, do me the favour.—Geſell, ' comrade,' is likewise a familiar and good-humoured appellation. Comp. 5, 207.

79. bürſten is provincially used in the sense of trinken. It would seem to have been originally a slang word in this sense.

80. Waſſerquell is a somewhat redundant compound, inasmuch as Quell of itself means a water-spring. But comp. v. 88, whence an argument may be derived why Uhland has expressly spoken of *water* here.

82. klar = rein.

83. bis oben = bis an ben Ranb, to the brim, v. 92.

95. We say more fully, von bieſer Stunbe an.

XVI.

The dynasty of the Hohenstaufen owed its destruction to the Papal power, which the Hohenstaufen Emperors had always opposed with all their might. Frederick II., who was only three years old at the death of his father (1197), was crowned at Aachen in 1215, and soon took up the policy of his family, which he continued during his whole reign. When Pope Gregory IX. convoked a council at Rome, Frederick's illegitimate son, Enzio or Hensius (i.e. Heinz, an abbreviated form of Heinrich), intercepted many of the bishops on their way, after a sharply contested naval battle with the Genoese fleet, A.D. 1241. Enzio's valour was henceforth of great assistance to his father, who honoured this favourite son with the royal title. But in 1249 Enzio was beaten by the Bolognese in the battle of Fossalta, and taken prisoner. "Les Ghibellins étaient conduits par le roi Hensius; chaque armée comptait de quinze à vingt mille combattants. La bataille fut longue et sanglante, mais elle se termina par la défaite complète des Ghibellins. Le roi Hensius tomba lui-même entre les mains des vainqueurs; il fut aussitôt conduit à Bologne et enfermé au palais du podestat. Le sénat de Bologne repoussa toute offre de rançon, toute intercession en sa faveur ; il pourvut d'une manière splendide à son entretien, mais il le retint captif pendant le reste de sa vie, qui dura encore vingt-deux ans." Simonde di Sismondi, *Histoire de la Renaissance de la liberté en Italie* (Paris, 1832), vol. I. p. 125. It was, therefore, Enzio's tragic fate to survive the extinction of all the rest of his family (Frederick II. Dec. 13, 1250; his son Conrad IV. 1254; Manfred was defeated and killed in the battle of Benevent 1266; Frederick's grandson Conradin was defeated at Tagliacozzo Aug. 23, 1268, and executed at the command of Charles d'Anjou, Oct. 29, 1268). When the news of Conradin's execution reached him, Enzio attempted an escape. "Pour mieux tromper la vigilance de ses geôliers, il se fit enfermer dans un tonneau que des hommes dévoués devaient faire sortir de Bologne sur un chariot chargé de marchandises ; mais au moment où ce précieux chariot allait dépasser la dernière porte de la ville, l'un des gardiens ayant aperçu une mèche de cheveux blonds qui s'échappait de l'une des fentes du tonneau, et s'étant écrié: 'Oh ! il n'y a que le roi Hensius qui puisse avoir de si beaux cheveux !' le pauvre prince fut découvert dans son étroite cachette, et ramené dans sa prison, où il mourut trois ans après, consumé d'ennuis et de regrets." Lamé-Fleury.

4. Aar is poetical instead of Adler.

5. Reno is the river on which Bologna is situated.

11. ob=obgleich, although. Comp. 40, 19.

21, 22. In prose: meine blutigrothe Thränen.

25. Unb ist=wenn wirklich mein Vater gestorben ist.

29. In poetry Mond is often used instead of Monat. The two words are originally identical. Comp. the Greek μήν and E. *moon.*

33 sq. Animate and inanimate nature is to participate in his grief.

36. Weisen, 'melodies,' in the same way as *modi* is used in Latin (*magna modis tenuare parvis*, Hor.).

38. It is more usual to say hervorloden.—There is a period to all complaints, just as nature does not always mourn in the garb of winter, but returns to new life in spring, I too may conceive new hopes, in spite of my glorious father's death.

39. His father had been designated as the Sun (19), his brothers—Conrad IV. in Germany, and Manfred in Sicily and Naples—are now styled stars.

40. mir, *dat. eth.* =meine Brüter.

44. Comp. Horace's expression, *lucida sidera*, likewise applied to two brothers.

47. The most usual form of this word is the plural die Trümmer; the singular is originally das Trumm, but is almost out of use nowadays; but the plural die Trümmer has erroneously been employed as a singular (as in this line) by many writers since Klopstock; nay, even der Trümmer occurs.

48. The preposition von is not employed here merely to replace the genitive, but denotes that which is *left of* the splendour of the house.

51. The expression sich mit Staub besäen is very bold, in the sense of sich mit Staub bedecken or bestreuen (besprengen). Grimm (*wörterb.* I, 1539) quotes from Jean Paul the expression sich mit Puder besäen, to bestrew one's hair with powder.

54. According to the ancient legend, Philomela was changed into a nightingale by mourning for the slaughter of Procne's child (Itys). See Ovid, *Met.* VI. 451 sqq.

57. Auen is here used in the wider sense of the word; see n. on 7, 10.

68. zum Königsfaal, so as to make it like a regal hall.

69. The usual form is verschönern.

70. rosiger Wein means merely red (or rosy) wine.

72. The sound of the harp goes forth into the land.

75. begraben is the infinitive, not the past participle.

76. Herzlieb (very frequently also in the diminutival form, Herzliebchen) = Eng. 'sweetheart.'

79. verbluten, to expire in bleeding. :

82. Die Treue, instead of der Treue = der Freund, v. 86.

96. Herzallerliebst, most dearly beloved.

98. In this style of poetry, the apocopated form Brüd' is rather harsh at the end of the line.

104. Observe the omission of the copula und. The songs are said to call back his friend and the merry old time.

109. The harp is the cause of the cheerful tone of Enzio's mind; the harp being dashed to pieces, his cheerfulness is likewise killed with grief.

111. Observe the difference between Kerkerhöhle here and Kerkerhaus above, v. 66.

112. Vertrauern, 'to waste (pine) away in mourning.'

118. Schwanenlied, the final song, shortly before death. It is an old belief that the dying swan breaks out into melodious singing.

119. Ade is a Germanized form of the French *adieu*, much used in poetry.

120. More strictly we ought to expect the perfect in this sentence, which is intended to express a final result, in much the same sense as jetzt ist der letzte Staube todt. But these two tenses are sometimes used promiscuously, particularly by natives of the South of Germany.

XVII.

The death of Conrad IV. (1254) was followed by what Schiller designates die kaiserlose, die schreckliche Zeit, commonly called the *Interregnum* in German history. This lawless period was auspiciously terminated by the election of *Rudolf von Habsburg* (or Hapsburg), A.D. 1273. His election took place at Frankfort-on-the-Maine, the coronation at Aachen. Rudolf was even before that time possessed of considerable power as count of Habsburg, Lenzburg, and Kyburg, and protector of numerous cities and districts.

In the present ballad Schiller's intention is to depict and exalt the virtue of Humility, even in the greatest of the land. The source of the tale is in the *Chronicon Helveticum* of Ægidius Tschudi (Götzinger, *Deutsche Dichter*, I. p. 398 sq.), and Schiller appears to have adhered, with much fidelity, to the original narrative.

1. Kaiſerpracht, 'imperial state.'

2. altertḧümlich, 'time-honoured' (lit. old-fashioned, antique).

3. König Rudolfs heilige Macht is said in imitation of such a Homeric expression as ίερὴ ἴς Τηλεμάχοιο. We might also say that Macht was here synonymous with the common term Majeſtät.

5 sq. "The office, at the coronation-feast, of the Count Palatine of the Rhine (Grand Sewer of the Empire and one of the Seven Electors) was to bear the Imperial Globe and set the dishes on the board; that of the King of Bohemia was cup-bearer. The latter was not, however, present, as Schiller himself observed in a note (omitted in the editions of his collected works), at the coronation of Rudolf." Lord Lytton.

6. des perlenten Weins is the partitive genitive, which is but rarely used in German without a preceding subst. or adj. Comp. Goethe's *Hermann and Dorothea*, I, 166: Sorgſam brachte tie Mutter des klaren herrlichen Weines.

8. ber Sterne Chor, the seven planets known in the Middle Ages.

9. According to mediæval notions, the Emperor was the temporal, and the Pope the spiritual ruler of the whole *orbis terrarum.* Comp. 7, 20, where the dying Emperor styles himself Herrſcher einer Welt.

10. üben, instead of the compound ausüben.

11. Balkón preserves its French accent even in German.

17. The Emperor was considered the highest judge in all temporal matters. Rudolf of Habsburg, in particular, was famous for his strict administration of justice.

21. Der Pokál, from *póculum,* always denotes a goblet of curious workmanship.

23. We might also say zwar instead of wohl, or the sentence might be turned thus: obwohl (obgleich) das Feſt glänzt..., (ſo) vermiſſe ich toch....

28. So hab' ich's gehalten, 'this custom have I observed.'

31. The princes form a circle around the Emperor.

32. ber Talár denotes a long robe that descends to the feet (*ad talos*).

35. ber Saiten Golb = tie goltenen Saiten. The strings are, however, only of the colour of gold.

36. Die Minne is a synonym of Liebe, but only admissible in the highest style of poetry. It is a mediæval word which had gone out of fashion, but was revived by the romantic school of poetry.

43. in Jemandes Pflicht ſtehen is not a common expression, meaning 'to be some one's liegeman.' The 'greater master' is, of course, the divine power by which all genuine poetry is inspired.

46. von wannen = woher.

49. The thoughts awakened by poetry are bunfel, 'secret,' because their existence was hitherto unknown to us; they are wunterbar, 'strange,' because their starting-up out of their sleep has a startling effect upon us.

51. In die Saiten fallen is not a common expression, though readily understood. We commonly say, rasch in die Saiten greifen.

53. Das Waidwerk is a dignified expression, instead of die Jagd.

54. flüchtig, fleet. It has been justly observed that it is a strange oversight on Schiller's part to send the Count a-hunting on horseback for chamois, since it is notorious that these fleet animals live on rocky heights inaccessible to horses.

57 sq. In the author followed by Schiller the expressions are as follows: *dero zeit reit graf Rudolf von Habsburg (harnach künig) mit sinen dienern uffs weidwerk…und wie er in ein ouw* (see our note on 7, 10) *kam allein mit seinem pferd, hört er ein schellen klingeln…dô fand er ein priester mit dem hochwürdigen sacrament und sin messner, der im das glögli* ('little bell') *vortrug. dô stieg graf Rudolf von sinem pferd, kniet nieder und tet dem heiligen Sacrament reverenz.* This passage may be sufficient to show how closely Schiller has followed his original.

59. Der Leib des Herrn: the host, which, according to Roman Catholic notions, represents the actual body and blood of the Lord. See also our note on 6, 51.

60. der Meßner, from Lat. *mansionarius* (in Middle High German it is *mensner* and *messenaere*), originally the doorkeeper of the Church.

64. erlöset: is this the present, or should we supply hat?

68. We should pronounce beiseit with the accent on the second syllable; the original form is bei (or zur) Seite legen.

70. In prose we should rather say, um das Bächlein zu durchschreiten.

71. Was schafft du? is said in accordance with the Swiss idiom, instead of was thust du da? In the South of Germany schaffen is often used as a synonym of arbeiten.

73. wallen is a very dignified expression, instead of ich wandere. There is always a notion of solemnity in this word.

74. Himmelskost, 'heavenly food,' denotes the sacrament.

75. des Baches Steg, the small bridge leading across the brook.

78. werte=zu Theil werte.—Heil, 'salvation.' We often read sein ewiges Heil.

79. Wässerlein, a small stream. The good priest purposely ex-

tenuates the size of the water, as if what he is about to do were nothing so very great after all.

83. begehren governs the genitive; see Aue § 349.

86. Die Begier des Jagens vergnügen is an expression admissible only in the elevated style of poetry. In prose we say sich mit etwas vergnügen.

89. Da is, properly speaking, unnecessary.

90. This line is often cited in German schools as an instance of a very loose participial construction. The poet's meaning is, of course, that the horse was modestly led by the bridle and not bestridden by the priest, but as the words stand now they might imply that the priest (who is the subject immediately preceding) was led by the bridle.

91. Nicht wolle das Gott, God forbid.—Demuthsfinn, a compound formed by Schiller, = demüthiger Sinn.

93. ein Roß beschreiten is a dignified expression, instead of ein Pferd besteigen, 'to bestride a horse.'

95. In prose: und wenn du es nicht als dein persönliches Eigenthum nehmen willst.—Der Gewinnst (or, as it ought rather to be spelt, Gewinst) is merely concrete, while der Gewinn is both concrete and abstract.

99. Das Lehen, 'a fief,' the word is connected with leihen, 'to lend.' The expression, zu Lehen tragen, is technical in the sense of 'holding' in fief.

101. So möge: we may observe that so, which is often used at the head of a wish, corresponds exactly to the Latin *sic* as seen in such a sentence as Horace's *sic te diva potens Cypri; sic fratres Helenae.*—Hort: see note on 4, 15.

103. The pronoun euch is emphatically repeated from the first line of the sentence, though, strictly speaking, unnecessary in this place.

106. ritterlich(es) Walten, knightly rule.

107 sqq. The six daughters of Rudolf were—(1) *Mechtilda*, subsequently consort to Ludwig, Duke of Bavaria; (2) *Agnes*, consort to Albrecht, Duke of Saxony; (3) *Hedwig*, consort to Otto of Brandenburg; (4) *Catharina*, consort to Otto, Duke of Bavaria; (5) *Gutta*, consort to Wenzel, king of Bohemia; (6) *Clementia*, consort to Charles Martel, prince of Sicily.

110. 'And may their latest generations still flourish.' The expression is not, however, quite clear in its grammatical construction, on account of the position of the verb, which ought rather to be after Geschlechter.

B.   9

111.   mit finnenbem $aupt = mit nachbenflich aufgeftü<u></u>tem $aupte.

113.   Observe the peculiar German construction, bem Sänger ins
Auge, instead of in bas Auge bes Sängers.

114.   Das Bebeuten is a poetical use of the infinitive instead of bie
Bebeutung.

116 sq.   Schiller has with much tact merely insinuated what the
original writer, Tschudi, has plainly stated in the following paragraph :
Der priester wird kaplan des churfürstlichen Ertzbischoffs von Mainz,
und hat im und andern herrn von solcher tugend, ouch von mannheit
des grafen Rudolf so dick (so much, greatly) *angezeigt, dass sîn nam im*
ganzen rîch rumwürdig und bekannt ward, dass er hernach ze römischen
künig erwelt ward.

118.   Alles = Alle.   The neut. sing. of the pronoun all is often used
of persons with a plural meaning.

120.   göttliches Walten, divine dispensation.

XVIII.

1.   *Germersheim* is a small town in the Palatinate, about two (German) miles' distance from Speyer, on the Rhine, and the Queich, a
small tributary.

4.   The game of chess is commonly denoted by the compound bas
Schachspiel.   Rudolf I. was very fond of this game (hence the adj.
gewohnt).

6.   ohne Zagen, without hesitation, i.e. plainly and to the point.

10.   Wohl, in all probability.

14.-   Observe the omission of hatte.   We might also say, beenbet
war.

15.   Eight German Emperors were originally buried in the ancient
Cathedral of Speyer (Conrad II., Heinrich III., IV., V., Philip of
Swabia, Rudolf of Habsburg, Adolf of Nassau, and Albrecht I.); but
their bones were impiously unearthed and dispersed by the French
invaders, May 31, 1689.

16.   fei's vollenbet, there let my course be finished !

27.   Kapellan is the original trisyllabic form, instead of which Kaplan
is now more usual.

28.   halb Leich(e), already half a corpse.

31.   The birds that have found shelter (Hut) in the branches of the
linden-tree.

33.   bes Wegs : for this use of the genitive see our note on 13, 45.

34. tie bange Sage, 'the anxious tale.' The 'tale' is styled bang, because the people whisper it to one another with fear and wonder.

35. Bilt, 'shape,' like the Greek εἶδος.

40. im Maien is poetical and archaic instead of in tem Mai.

46. rasch denotes the last effort made by the Emperor. He musters up strength sufficient to enter the Imperial hall with a quick and active step. Comp. 7, 36.

49. Der heil'ge Leib: comp. 17, 59.

51. sich verjüngen means to grow young again.

55. entschlummert, like entschlafen, 'slept away,' is often used of peaceful and quiet dying.

58. The expression zur Leiche bieten is the technical term of inviting to a funeral. Hence the man whose business it is to do this is styled ter Leichenbitter.

62. The people, black, in a countless throng. For this use of the genitive comp. Es wallt ein Pilger, hohen Dranges. Uhland.

63. Der, i.e. ter Dom.

64. The expression ter Dom des Himmels is by no means uncommon, even in the higher style of prose. Comp. the beautiful lines of Thümmel, quoted by Grimm, *wörterb.* 2, 1234:

> Wenn aufgeschwungen aus tem Schlamme
> Des Irtischen mein freier Geist
> Von einem zu tem antern Dome
> Der Sterngebäute weiter klimmt.

XIX.

The subject of the present ballad is taken from the events which happened in the reign of the Emperor *Albrecht* (1298—1308), the son of Rudolf of Habsburg. After Rudolf's death, the Electors had chosen Adolphus of Nassau to be his successor, who reigned from 1292—1298. Adolphus chiefly aimed at enlarging his own territorial possessions; by promising to assist Edward I. of England against Philip le Bel of France, he obtained considerable subsidies from the English king, and this money he employed to purchase Thuringia from the landgrave then reigning there, *Albrecht*, an unworthy man whom history has branded with the disgraceful addition ter Unartige, or *degener* in Latin. Albrecht by his cruelty had driven away his excellent wife, *Margaretha*, daughter of Frederick II., the famous Hohenstaufen Emperor ; when the poor lady was obliged to leave the Wartburg (near Eisenach), she is said to have bitten her boy's cheek in the excessive grief of leaving him ; hence he bears in history the name of Friedrich mit der gebiſſenen Wange. The *unkind* father, who had taken a second wife, Kunigunde von Eisenberg, sold his land in order to deprive his sons by the first wife, *Friedrich* and *Diezmann*, of their inheritance. Meanwhile the conduct of Adolphus had excited general disgust. The German princes declared that he had forfeited his dignity, and elected in his stead *Albrecht* of Habsburg. But the two brothers were not freed from their troubles by this change. Adolphus fell fighting against his rival in the battle of Göllheim ; but Albrecht himself renewed his predecessor's pretensions to Thuringia, on the plea that the purchase had been made in favour of the Imperial throne, and not of the then occupant of it. Friedrich and Diezmann fought manfully for their paternal estate. The present poem relates one of the episodes of the war. It terminated in the complete defeat of the Imperial troops in the battle of Lucka (not far from Altenburg) on May 31, 1307.

4. ſich ſchirmen = ſich vertheidigen is peculiar to an elevated style.

8. verlaufen is used in a somewhat loose manner here, inasmuch as Albrecht *sold* his land, properly speaking ; but the Pope and Habsburg contributed to the bargain being carried out.—ihm is dat. comm.

10. Lande is a poetical form of the plural instead of Länder.

15. This may be an allusion to Luther's subsequent residence at the Wartburg, during which he commenced his translation of the Bible.

. 18. übermannen, originally 'to bear down by force of numbers,' hence generally to conquer, vanquish.

21. The expression über Stock und Stein is proverbial of hurried progress, regardless of bad roads and other obstacles. Observe the alliterative form of this phrase.

22. In prose : um der Gefangenſchaft bei dem Kaiſer zu entgehen.

23. In prose : Der Landgraf iſt allein (einzig) darauf bedacht, etc.

29. Reichspanier, the Imperial standard.

33. The phrase Sand am Meer is proverbial of an immense multitude. It is of biblical origin, comp. Psalm cxxxix. 18 : Sollte ich ſie zählen, ſo würde ihrer mehr ſein denn des Sandes, and 1 Kings iv. 29 :

Gott gab Salomo sehr große Weisheit und Verstand, und getrost Herz, wie Sand, der am Ufer des Meeres liegt. Comp. also ballad 30, 6.

37. schlecht and schlicht (= E. *slight*) were originally one and the same word; hence the phrase schlecht und recht, 'simple and right.' In the present passage, ein schlechtes Bauernhaus means a cottage of poor appearance.

40. mir is 'dat. ethicus' or 'commodi,' in English to be translated by adding the possessive pronoun to Knaben.—stillen, to quiet, hence to suckle.

41. Derweil (originally a genitive, der Weile), 'meanwhile.' Comp. 5, 210.—In prose we should have to say, wendet er sein Pferd um.

45. voller is a conversational and poetical form instead of voll when used like a preposition.

51. The genitive des Landgrafs is not correct; it ought to be des Landgrafen.

XX.

The period from the thirteenth to the sixteenth century was the one most favourable to the growth of the power of the princes and nobles, and embraces the decay of the once powerful Imperial dignity. The sole aim of the Emperors of this time appears to have been to augment and increase their own family estates, while they cared little for the Empire as such. We shall, therefore, now turn our attention to the condition of the separate states of the German Empire. Ballads XX. and XXI. contain two episodes of the history of the Empire during this period of misrule.

Count Eberhard II. of Würtemberg reigned from 1344 to 1392 conjointly with his brother Ulrich IV. who died in that year without leaving an heir. Eberhard was surnamed der Greiner, i.e. the quarreller. His lot was cast in a most disturbed period. The Swabian cities, encouraged by the example of the Swiss, attempted to shake off the yoke of their prince, and the lower nobility were likewise astir to free themselves of their duty and allegiance. The Emperors of this period, Charles IV., Wenceslaus, and Ruprecht, possessed little or no authority, and Eberhard was obliged to stand by himself against all his enemies. Uhland has related some of the memorable events of Eberhard's reign in a series of ballads, from which we have selected a poetical account of the battle of Reutlingen, May 14, 1377. Eberhard was engaged in the siege of Ulm, and had ordered his son Ulrich to blockade the city of Reutlingen, near which the castle of Achalm is situated.

3. Flügel is a very appropriate expression in this place, being employed both of birds and of armies, like the E. *wing*. (There is, however, another reading Flüge.)

4. heißer Drang here = heißes Bedrängtwerten. The town was being hard pressed.

5. sich erheben = aufbrechen, sich aufmachen.—zu Nacht is less common than bei Nacht or zur Nachtzeit.

6. Urach is a fortified town on the river Erms, to the east of Reutlingen.

8. Observe the omission of the verb sind or werten. This is very frequent in a lively description.

9. The more common expression is grimmiger Zorn.

12. zuthal, down the mountain, comp. Fr. *à val*.

13. Leonhard is always pronounced as three syllables.

14. Anger is best translated by 'a common.' The derivation of the word is anything but clear.

15. We say 'they draw *out* their proud array.'

19. fürter, an archaic word, = vorwärts. Comp. 9. 30.

23. Die Rotte is frequently used in the sense of the E. *crew*, when not employed of sailors, with a certain notion of disorder and turbulence. Here it means merely the subdivisions of the town forces.— Schwall suggests the idea of rising waters that dash against rocks and walls.

27. schier, see 5, 69.

31 sq. The town of Reutlingen is famous for its tanyards and dyeing works.

33. Heut' nimmt man nicht gefangen, no quarter is given to-day.

34. sich blümen = sich mit Blumen bedecken, not a common expression. Grimm, *wörterb.* 2, 161, quotes only one instance from Voss: wie tort grünentes Thal sich blümet.

36. Bruderleichen: the bodies of their fallen and slain friends and comrades lie around the surviving knights in such high heaps as to form a kind of tower (umthürmt). (The compound Bruderleiche is omitted in Grimm.)

38. The expression bis in's (innerste) Mark müte is proverbial.

40. We also say, sich durchhauen or durchschlagen.—Uhland alludes to an ancient legend, according to which two brothers, Egino and Rudolf, rebuilt the castle of Achalm in the reign of the Emperor Conrad, 1006. When Rudolf asked his dying brother what name he was to give the Castle, he answered *Ach Allm—*, intending to say *Allmächtiger*, but his voice was stopped by death. Rudolf, however, called the castle

Achalm in memory of his brother. In reality, the name of *Achalm* is equivalent in meaning to 𝔚𝔞𝔰𝔰𝔢𝔯𝔞𝔩𝔭𝔢 (*aha* being old German = Latin *aqua*). Comp. 7, 10.

43. 𝔇𝔢𝔯 𝔔𝔲𝔞𝔩𝔪 is rarely used in the meaning, 'a fainting-fit,' or 'a kind of stupor.' Comp. Middleton's play, *A Mad World* (Dodsley, vol. II. p. 330, ed. 1826), 'a fit, a qualm.'

47. 𝔤𝔢𝔯𝔢𝔦𝔥𝔱 = in 𝔑𝔢𝔦𝔥' 𝔲𝔫𝔡 𝔊𝔩𝔦𝔢𝔡 𝔞𝔲𝔰𝔤𝔢𝔩𝔢𝔤𝔱.

48. 𝔪𝔦𝔱 𝔰𝔦𝔠𝔥𝔢𝔯𝔢𝔪 𝔊𝔢𝔩𝔢𝔦𝔱, with a safe conduct.

49. 𝔡𝔢𝔫𝔫 is occasionally used instead of 𝔞𝔩𝔰 after a comparative.

59. 𝔤𝔢𝔩𝔞𝔰𝔰𝔢𝔫, instead of 𝔩𝔬𝔰𝔤𝔢𝔩𝔞𝔰𝔰𝔢𝔫 or 𝔣𝔞𝔥𝔯𝔢𝔫 𝔩𝔞𝔰𝔰𝔢𝔫.

61. 𝔖𝔠𝔥𝔦𝔩𝔡𝔢𝔰𝔞𝔪𝔱 = 𝔑𝔦𝔱𝔱𝔢𝔯𝔰𝔠𝔥𝔞𝔣𝔱.

63. The royal house of Prussia are descended from the counts of Zollern.

64. 𝔦𝔪 𝔨ü𝔫𝔣𝔱'𝔤𝔢𝔫 𝔊𝔩𝔞𝔫𝔷, in the splendour which was to *come* to it.

65. 𝔷𝔴𝔢𝔢𝔫, archaic for 𝔷𝔴𝔢𝔦 (comp. Eng. *twain*), often used in Luther's Bible: see Luke xxiv.' 13.

66. This is an allusion to the arms of the knights of Sachsenheim.

71. 𝔊𝔢𝔰𝔠𝔥𝔩𝔢𝔠𝔥𝔱𝔢, instead of 𝔊𝔢𝔰𝔠𝔥𝔩𝔢𝔠𝔥𝔱, produces a somewhat strange and affected impression.

72. 𝔦𝔫𝔰 𝔥𝔢𝔯𝔷, i.e. death struck him home, so that he cannot come back like his ancestor.

73. The partitive genitive 𝔡𝔢𝔰 𝔍𝔞𝔪𝔪𝔢𝔯𝔰 is dependent on 𝔤𝔢𝔫𝔲𝔤 : *satis miseriarum.*

77. 𝔞𝔲𝔰𝔤𝔢𝔥𝔢𝔦𝔩𝔱 means 'completely healed.'

78. Ulrich guessed what welcome he would meet with from his father.

79. The preposition 𝔟𝔢𝔦 would, perhaps, be more generally used in the phrase 𝔈𝔦𝔫𝔢𝔫 𝔟𝔢𝔦𝔪 𝔈𝔰𝔰𝔢𝔫 𝔱𝔯𝔢𝔣𝔣𝔢𝔫.

83. This peculiar treatment was not uncommon in the middle ages in the case of knights who were deemed to have disgraced their standard or been remiss in their duty. The table-cloth was cut through for them, and their bread was laid upside down.

XXI.

Count *Eberhard im Bart*, who was born in 1445, succeeded to the inheritance of his ancestors in 1457, under the guardianship of the Emperor Frederick III. He is considered one of the best rulers that his country ever had, and was greatly beloved by his subjects. He died in 1496. He was raised to the ducal dignity by the Emperor Maxi-

milian I.   The subject of the present ballad is derived from Camera-
rius's life of Melanchthon (Götzinger, *Deutsche Dichter*, I. p. 670).

4.   The diet held at Worms in 1495 is the one alluded to in the
present poem.

15.   Schaffen = bewirken, bring about.   See 17, 71.

16.   In prose the order of words would be—an Schätzen wohl nicht
nachsteht.

22.   This would in prose be expanded into a qualifying sentence:
wenn sie auch noch so groß sind.

23.   kühnlich is the adv. of kühn.

24.   In prose it would necessarily be in den Schooß, and even as it
is, the omission of the article appears to be rather harsh.

28.   Edelstein should be understood in the collective sense.

XXII.

The Emperor Maximilian (or, as he was commonly called, Max) I.
was, perhaps, the most popular prince of the House of Habsburg.   His
chivalrous qualities, and his bold, daring character endeared him to high
and low.   The Austrian poet, Anastasius Grün, has celebrated a number
of Max's exploits in a series of ballads, entitled Der letzte Ritter, and one
of these we have inserted in our collection.   The event related in it is
said to have taken place at the same diet as the one mentioned in the
preceding poem.

1.   Frederick III., the father and predecessor of Maximilian I.,
reigned from 1440 to 1493.—Gruft, a more dignified expression than
Grab, is frequently employed of princely sepulchres.

2.   gülten is archaic instead of golten.—Sonnenaar, the eagle that
soars aloft towards the sun.—Glück zu and Glück auf, 'good speed.'—
Scepter, here neuter as usually.   Compare, however, note on 7, 57.

4.   Licht is used metaphorically of mental culture, comp. the Fr.
les lumières.

6.   Otem is archaic instead of Athem.

8.   It was customary for princes of that time to keep privileged
court-jesters.

10.   Gartenreich, the kingdom of his garden.   The gardener puts his
garden in order and is there 'monarch of all he surveys.'

11.   erkoren, see note on 4, 12.—Schattenhut is an uncommon compound, instead of which we should probably say in prose, in dessen
behütendem Schatten.

12. It is not the toil (Mühe) which is ſchwül of itſelf, but the work is difficult on account of the sultry heat (ſchwül) of the day.

13. waſſen is here used in the sense of walking slowly. See 17, 73.—ein unb auß, 'up and down'; that is, they entered one street (ein) and walked down to the end of it until they got into another (auß).

16. traun (connected with the adj. treu and the verb trauen) is sometimes used in familiar speech as a kind of interjection with an affirmative sense: 'surely, to be sure.' Comp. 'I trow' in ballad-poetry.—manch einer corresponds exactly to '*many a one*'; it is, however, a provincial idiom in German, instead of the simple mancher.

18. The line will be readily understood in its application to French pronunciation.

19. ſeßen is used in the same sense as when we say 'to *set* a song to music.'

23. Schnörkelzüge is almost equivalent in sense to the simple Schnörkel, or to verſchnörkelte Züge, flourishes.

24. Schrieb, instead of hat er eingeſchrieben. This employment of the imperfect instead of the perfect is anything but correct.

25. i.e. jedem, der es lieſt.

26. kampfeßfroh = kampfbegierig. There is also the form kampffroh.

27. magſt bu = kannſt bu. This is the original sense of mögen (still perceptible in the compound vermögen), which is in modern German admissible in an elevated style or in poetry.

28. Rübe originally means 'a strong hound.' Ein Rübenknecht is, therefore, a groom of the kennel.

29. fürter. See note on 20, 19.

30. Edelknappe, a page of noble parentage. Grimm has only Edel-knabe.—In prose we should say bas Wappenbild ('the armorial bearings') ter Habsburger.

31. For the term Kampfeßplan, comp. our note on 4, 39. Grimm gives only an instance of Kampfplan.

32. Der Franke is often used in German instead of ter Franzoſe (see our note on Schiller's *Maid of Orleans*, Prol. 3, 126). Hence also the adj. fränkiſch = franzöſiſch. The expression Franzmann, employed in the next line, is generally used in a contemptuous sense.

35. verklärt, 'surrounded with a halo.'

36. See Rev. xii. 7.

40. The technical expression is (Einen) zum Ritter ſchlagen, to dub knight.—brav stands in the same sense as in French: *soyez brave*.

42. Frauen is here gen. sing. (referring to the Virgin Mary): comp. 15, 13, also Aue § 157.   The wine in question is actually called Liebfrauenmilch.

45. an Maxens Abendtisch = an der kaiserlichen Tafel zu Abend.

48. Glühborn, a word probably invented by the poet, means 'a warm spring' (Born = *burn*, i.e. running water), and is intended to denote the glowing wine.

51. mit jemanten anbinten, to pick a quarrel with some one.

53. Klangen die Becher, an allusion to the German custom of striking the glasses gently together to produce a ringing sound when drinking to the health of anyone.

54. genüber, a poetical form instead of gegenüber.

56. We have here a shortened conditional sentence, instead of wenn man am Morgen...frug, if indeed the question was put to the two.—selber, instead of selbst; this is a popular form, which should be avoided in careful prose-composition.

XXIII.

Georg von Frundsberg was one of the foremost generals of the early part of the reign of Charles V.   He subsequently assisted at the sack of Rome by the Imperial troops under the command of the famous Connétable de Bourbon.

3. The addition of the article before the proper name is a peculiarity of popular speech, and is avoided in careful composition, unless with an adjective (e. g. den berühmten Luther).

6. Close to the place where Luther was to enter the hall.

13. kühngestaltig is an adjective readily understood, but not in common use. (It is omitted in Grimm.) In prose we should say mit kühnen Gestalten.

19. True faith is like steel-armour or a breast-plate; hence the expression stählt instead of the simple and commonplace stärkt.

28. Die Losung is the watchword, a term used by Luther in his translation of the Bible, Judges xx. 38, and 2 Macc. xiii. 15. The expression is probably derived from an old word losen, 'to hear,' and would thus seem to be connected with the E. *listen*.

30. Frommverwegen might also be written as two words, the first part being adverbial, 'daring in piety.'

31. der Himmelserbe, 'heir of heaven,' an appellation given to Luther, a one who fights for the cause of Heaven and true religion, and may therefore be deemed sure to inherit the kingdom of Heaven.

33. Mönchlein, 'frail monk.' The diminutive is expressive of the insignificance or weakness of Luther's person when compared with the formidable array of power with which he is called upon to struggle.

34. Observe the so-called *figura etymologica* in the phrase einen Gang gehen.

35. Schlachtgewitter is a compound readily understood, and das Wetter der Schlacht would be admissible even in prose.

39. Mit Einem im Reinen sein is properly used of having cast up and settled one's accounts with some one.

41. Degen has been explained in a previous note (5, 37). Der greise Degen is, therefore, synonymous with der alte Held or Ritter.

48. Comp. the expression Flammenschwert, 22, 36.

XXIV.

Luther died Feb. 18, 1546, and was saved by death from witnessing the great calamities that befell the cause of the Protestants. On July 20th of the same year, the Elector of Saxony and the Landgrave of Hesse, the two most powerful princes of the Protestant party, were declared rebels and outlawed by the Emperor Charles V., and on April 24th of the ensuing year the army of the Elector was completely routed near Mühlberg. As Charles threatened to kill the Elector, the gates of the capital, Wittenberg, were opened to the enemy, in order to save his life. Then it was that the memorable scene took place, when the Duke of Alva pressed Charles to have Luther's bones disinterred from their resting-place in the *Schlosskirche*, whereupon Charles is said to have replied with the reproof related in the present poem.

1. Luthersfeste may be understood in a twofold sense, (1) as the fortified town in which Luther lived, (2) the centre from which his doctrine spread over all Germany.

2. Instead of der Sieger we should prefer in prose als Sieger.

3. For the construction of this line and the following we refer to our note on 15, 17.

5. The student should consider why Luthers Feste is here spelt as two words, but as one in v. 1.

8. billig, with justice, fittingly.

10. Auf denn corresponds to the Fr. *eh bien.*

11. For the phrase etwas preisgeben, see our note on Kohlrausch, p. 33, 3.

XXV.

On Sept. 7, 1556, Charles V., worn out with toil and disappoint-
ment, abdicated and in 1557 retired to the monastery of San Yuste, near
Placenzia, in the West of Spain. The arrival of Charles at the gate of
the monastery is the scene imagined by the poet: it is a stormy night,
nature suiting the aspect of the worn-out Emperor's mind.   The
monarch's only request is for quiet and solitude in which to await his
death.   Charles V. died on Sept. 21, 1558.

   1. für und für, 'without ceasing, incessantly.'

   2. Hispanisch is more stately, because more uncommon than the
ordinary adj. spanisch.

   6. "Charles had no relish for amusements of any kind. He endeavoured to conform, in his manner of living, to all the rigour of
monastic austerity. He desired no other society than that of monks,
and was almost continually employed with them in chanting the hymns
of the missal. As an expiation for his sins, he gave himself the discipline
in secret with such severity, that the whip of cords which he employed
as the instrument of his punishment was found after his decease tinged
with his blood. Nor was he satisfied with these acts of mortification,
which, however severe, were not unexampled. He resolved to celebrate
his own obsequies before his death. He ordered his tomb to be erected
in the chapel of the monastery. His domestics marched thither in
funeral procession, with black tapers in their hands....He himself followed in his shroud. He was laid in his coffin [Sarkophag] with much
solemnity. The service for the dead was chanted. This affected him
so much, that next day he was seized with a fever. His feeble frame
could not long resist its violence." Robertson, *Life of Charles V.,*
book XII. (p. 580 sq. in the Paris edition of 1828).

   8. Charles V. held the crowns of Germany, the Netherlands,
Austria, Spain, Naples, and Sicily, together with the new world discovered by Columbus.

   9. sich bequemen is an elegant expression in the sense of submitting
to something. Comp. Fr. *s'accommoder.*

   10. betiademen is not a common word, though easily intelligible:
'to diadem.' Grimm quotes only the present instance of this expression.

   14. Charles V. was indeed the last Emperor that attempted to
reassert the ancient prerogatives of the Imperial station, and to reduce
the overbearing vassals, who had become independent and powerful

princes, to the position of mere servants of the crown. It is true that the existence of the 'Empire' was protracted for another 250 years, but it was a mere name, without any living reality, εἴδωλον ἀμαυρόν. The 'ancient Empire' was indeed buried with Charles V. This dissolution and dismemberment was, if possible, carried still further by the most destructive war in the history of Germany, the Thirty Years War,

XXVI.

· The most striking figure among the warriors and generals of the Thirty Years' War is that of Wallenstein, whom Schiller has made the central figure of a noble trilogy. Originally a simple nobleman, *Albrecht von Waldstein*, he had been raised to the dignity of duke, and enriched with the domains of Friedland, in the North of Bohemia. After beating the Protestants, headed by King Christian IV. of Denmark, Wallenstein turned all his forces against the city of Stralsund, the only place in Germany that continued to hold out against his victorious army. The citizens defended themselves so manfully that Wallenstein was at length obliged to raise the siege, after having uselessly sacrificed 12,000 soldiers in repeated assaults, and though he had sworn to take the town 'even if it were chained to the heavens.' The memory of the siege is still kept up by the citizens of Stralsund in an annual festival celebrated on July 24th.

4. Die alte Riesin, the giant oak.

11 sq. Properly speaking, the sword which he holds in his right hand digs up the sandy soil.

15. Deß (=deſſen) is the demonstrative pronoun.

20. Stralsund is surrounded with water on all sides, and connected with the main land by means of three bridges. "Stralsund...est la plus forte place de la Poméranie. Elle est bâtie entre la mer Baltique et le lac de Franken, sur le détroit de Gella : on n'y peut arriver de terre que sur une chaussée étroite, défendue par une citadelle et par des retranchements qu'on croyait inaccessibles." Voltaire, *Charles XII*, livre huitième.

28. The usual expression is hervorſprühen.

29 sqq. The citizens of Stralsund were supported by reinforcements sent from Sweden and Denmark.

36. The expression Himmelszelt occurs also in 8, 12.

40. Ge-zweig has a collective sense, imparted to the original word Zweig by the prefix ge-.

49. Was iſt's? 'what can this be?' Wallenstein endeavours to make light of the warning whispered to him by the tree, but for all that his mind is accessible to superstitious impressions. So also v. 65.

54. The phrase es gilt points to the object for the accomplishment of which the toast is drunk. 'Here's to the fall of the fortress!' See also 8, 11.

56. Meeresflut means merely the waves of the sea; there being no ebb and flow of the tide in the Baltic.

57. See note on 22, 53.

61. The expression is intentionally repeated from v. 45. Comp. also v. 97.

67. geſchäftig, instead of eilig.

73. bedächtig is the opposite of heftig, v. 65; cf. the equivalent expression mit gutem Bedacht, 13, 47.

75 sq. In prose we should be obliged to say und bei dem Klange lachte Wallenſtein mächtig auf.

82. Umzuckte = flashed around. Comp. 40, 7.

83. Der Eiſenball is a poetical expression (omitted in Grimm) instead of the commonplace Kanonenkugel.

88. A capital illustration of the proverb 'there's many a slip 'twixt the cup and the lip,' or the Greek πολλὰ μεταξὺ πέλει κύλικος καὶ χείλεος ἄκρου.

92. His cheek had turned pale with fright at the sudden shock.

103. Compare Schiller's lines:

mit des Geſchickes Mächten
Iſt kein ew'ger Bund zu flechten,
Und das Unglück ſchreitet ſchnell.

104. nimmer is a stronger negation than nicht, or keinen Krieg. Comp. also 13, 15.

105. In prose: Wir ziehen von der Feſtung ab.

110. This is an allusion to the annual festivity mentioned in our introductory remarks.

XXVII.

The 'Great Elector,' Frederick William, Elector of Brandenburg and Duke of Prussia (1640—1688), stands at the beginning of a new epoch. The house of Habsburg, though still honoured with the Imperial name, had already sufficiently proved how little mindful it was of the true interests of the German nation, and how incapable of protecting German honour and dignity. While the Emperor quietly yielded up German territory to the encroachments of Louis XIV., the overbearing king of France, the Great Elector stood on the banks of the Rhine, doing his duty as a prince of the Empire and fighting against Turenne. In order to free himself from this valiant adversary, the French king caused the Swedes, his allies, to invade the domains of the Elector. The Swedes were burning and ravaging the districts of the Neumark, when the Elector suddenly appeared, after a rapid march, and beat the enemy (who was not prepared for his sudden appearance) in the glorious battle of *Fehrbellin.* The army of the Elector consisted of 5000 cavalry, while the hostile army numbered 11,000 men.

The event which forms the subject of our ballad is related by Frederick the Great, in his *Mémoires pour servir à l'histoire de la maison de Brandebourg,* in the following terms:

"Il est digne de la majesté de l'histoire de rapporter la belle action que fit un écuyer de l'électeur dans ce combat. L'électeur montait un cheval blanc: Froben, son écuyer, s'aperçut que les Suédois tiraient plus sur ce cheval qui se distinguait par sa couleur, que sur les autres; il pria son maître de le troquer contre le sien, sous prétexte que celui de l'électeur était ombrageux; et à peine ce fidèle domestique l'eut-il monté quelques moments qu'il fut tué, et sauva ainsi par sa mort la vie à l'électeur."

It should, however, be added that this story, in spite of the authority of Frederick the Great, has no actual foundation, and may be treated as a mere legend.

3. The *Rhin* is a small river in the Mark.

5. The expression noch mehr denotes that the Swedes had obtained a considerable portion of Pomerania in the Westphalian peace (1648).

8. The river Oder discharges its waters into the Baltic by three different channels, called *Peene, Swine,* and *Dievenow.* The *Peene* formed in those days the frontier between Sweden and Prussia.

9. Count Gustavus Wrangl was the Swedish commander.

11. The more usual phrase is jeber Art.

13. traun, 'to be sure'; see n. on 22, 16.

16. nicht aus Scheuen, not out of fear. Comp. the phrase, er scheut bas Feuer, he is afraid of fire.

18. The preposition zu is generally added, when rufen is construed with the dative.—Soldiers are often addressed as Kinter by a popular commander.

20. geschieht = gerichtet wird (sc. bas Schießen).

21. The contraction Schlecht's instead of Schlechtes is somewhat harsh, but in the style of popular poetry.

23. The famous general of the Elector mentioned in the present line is commonly styled ter alte Dörflinger.

27. weichet, in the sense of the Fr. *reculez, retirez*, to which zurück is commonly added in German.

28. ter gleiche = sich stets gleiche, undisturbed.

29. mochte es ahnen = 'probably had a presentiment.'

32. gangen instead of gegangen, is another peculiarity of popular speech. Comp. also 12, 9.

33. The fate of Prussia seemed at that critical moment to depend on the accurate aim of a Swedish soldier.

35. Frederick, the son of the Great Elector, was crowned king of Prussia at Königsberg in 1701. He reigned from 1688—1713.

36. An Elector wore in token of his dignity a peculiarly shaped *hat* or cap of scarlet trimmed with ermine.

39. The prince of Homburg was one of the Great Elector's generals; he was noted for his impetuosity (Hitze) and nearly lost his life for allowing his rashness to carry him away so far as to counteract the express orders of the Elector. See H. von Kleist's tragedy, Prinz Friedrich von Homburg.

41. Death is often compared to a reaper. Comp. our note on Kohlrausch, p. 66, 4.

42. Alles = Alle. See note on 17, 118.

46. Gewehr is used in the wider sense of 'artillery.'

48. zurecht reiten = zureiten, 'to break in' (of a horse).

49. In prose: zu ihm herüber.—Lieblingsroß, 'favourite horse.' We have elsewhere spoken of the compounds formed with Liebling, and their correspondence with the adj. *favourite*.

52. ten Zügel lang verhänget : comp. 4, 82.

59. Der Schimmel setzt hoch auf = bäumt sich hoch auf.

60. According to strict grammar, we should expect the plural of the verb after two subjects. But this rule is by no means invariably observed in German.

61. Ritter denotes the noble cavaliers, and not exactly 'knights.' The time of mediæval knighthood had long since passed by.

63. Ha! expresses the Elector's surprise when he understands Froben's generous intention.

XXVIII.

"L'année 1717, le prince Eugène assiégea Belgrade, dans laquelle il y avait près de quinze mille hommes de garnison; il se vit lui-même assiégé par une armée innombrable de Turcs qui avançaient contre son camp et qui l'environnèrent de tranchées ; il était précisément dans la situation où se trouva César en assiégeant Alexie ; il s'en tira comme lui ; il battit les ennemis et prit la ville ; toute son armée devait périr ; mais la discipline militaire triompha de la force et du nombre." Voltaire, *Siècle de Louis XV*, p. 4 éd. de Basle (1785). Eugene's splendid victory was celebrated in the popular song which we have likewise inserted in the present collection. Freiligrath's poem is intended to suggest a scene which may have taken place at the time of the composition of the spirited Volkslied which has not lost anything of its vitality after the lapse of more than a century and a half.

1. Wer da? 'who's there?' is the cry of the sentinels.

6. In prose: schwere Karabiner.

9. Das Piket, a French expression like most military terms, instead of the German die Feldwache.

14. The dative Decken is antiquated, instead of Decke. See also Aue § 137, note, and compare the phrases auf Erden, zu Ehren, von Seiten.

16. Die Knöchel denotes the dice (Würfel) which are made of bone.

19. Affaire is often used of a battle.

20. We often say, zu Nutz und Frommen, 'for the benefit of.......'

23. Weißen und Rothen denotes the different uniforms of the Imperial troops. The general uniform of the Austrian army is white.

27. Denen is archaic instead of den.—Reitersleute is the plural of Reitersmann.

34. thät streichen is in the popular style instead of er strich, comp. 13, 26.

XXIX.

In the 'Volkslied' we notice very many antiquated expressions. We shall merely give their modern equivalents.

2. wied'rum kriegen = wieder erwerben.

3. Belgarad is a lengthened form instead of the usual Belgrad.

4. einen Brucken = eine Brücke.

5. kunnt' = konnte.—rucken = rücken.

6. für = vor. In the language of the seventeenth century the two prepositions für and vor were used quite promiscuously.

8. Stuck = Stück or Stück(en), field-piece, cannon.

10. Observe the careless rhyme or rather assonance in Lager and

verjagen. Such negligent rhymes are quite in the style of popular poetry. Others of the same kind occur further on in 'the poem.

16. futragiren instead of fouragiren, possibly with some reference to the German word Futter.

21. Seine General instead of Generäle.

22. inftrugiren = inftruiren. The plebeian dialect adds the letter g in order to avoid the hiatus.

24. recht, i. e. in ter richtigen Weife.

25. Bei ter Parole, when the *parole*, i. e. the watchword of the day was given out.

29. fcharmützen is a word peculiar to the soldier's language: the proper word being fcharmützeln. Comp. the Fr. *escarmoucher.*

28 sq. Alles...was instead of Alle...welche. The neuter of the pronoun is often used to denote persons collectively. (17, 118; 27, 42.)

33. Schanz = Schanze.

44. als wie = gerate wie. It is not considered correct to employ als wie in good writing, though it is often heard in conversation.

46. There is no prince *Ludwig* known as having fought at the siege of Belgrade. Eugene's brother in arms was Prince Ludwig von Baden, who was not, however, present on this occasion.

47. Halt't instead of haltet would be inadmissible in correct writing.

XXX.

The splendid victory of Leuthen was won by Frederick the Great over the Austrians on Dec. 5, 1757. The event related in the present poem is recorded by Mr Carlyle in the following characteristic manner :

"Thick darkness; silence; tramp, tramp,—a Prussian grenadier broke out, with solemn tenor voice again, into Church-Music; a known Church-Hymn, of the homely *Te Deum* kind, in which five-and-twenty thousand other voices, and all the regimental bands, soon join—

> Nun tanket Alle Gott,
> Mit Herzen, Mund und Händen,
> Der große Dinge thut
> An uns und aller Enden.

> Now thank God, one and all,
> With heart, with voice, with hands—a,
> Who wonders great hath done
> To us and to all lands--a.

And thus they advance; melodious, far-sounding, through the hollow night, once more in a highly remarkable manner. A pious people, of right Teutsch stuff, tender though stout; and, except perhaps Oliver Cromwell's handful of Ironsides, probably the most perfect soldiers ever seen hitherto." *Frederick the Great*, book XVIII. chap. X. (p. 277 of the Leipzig reprint).

2. das Kaiserheer = das kaiserliche Heer, the Imperial army (of Maria Theresa).

3. Observe the omission of the verb ist in the relative sentence.

4. The fearful work done during the day is being covered up with the veil night throws over it.

5. Licht is used in the sense of Stern. Comp. Genesis i. 14 : und Gott sprach: Es werden Lichter an der Veste des Himmels. The expression, Sand am Meer in the following line is likewise biblical.

10. Gelag, 'feasting.'

13. entquellen is originally used of a well or spring breaking forth with might; it is then metaphorically employed of singing, and even of strong powerful speaking and declamation.—er singt fort, 'goes on singing.'

17. Es strömt = das Volk (das Heer) strömt (zusammen).

18. Einfallen is the technical term for joining in a song.

19. feiern, 'to be lazy, be behindhand, or backward.'

20. Pronounce Hobó. The original form is Hoboe.

21. What had originally been a mere river (Strom) increases to the size of the sea.

22. rings = ringsum, all around (in a ring).

23. The valley, which had already composed itself to quiet and repose, is wakened up by the singing of the army and re-echoes with the solemn chant.

24. Pronounce Chorál, with the accent on the second syllable. This is originally an adj. in Latin, *carmen chorale*, a lay sung by a choir.

XXXI.

The anecdote which has furnished the subject of this ballad is well known. We may add that Frederick II. or the Great, built the palace of Sanssouci in the years 1745—1747, and that the windmill which the obstinate owner refused to give up to the royal bidder is still in existence and still belongs to the descendants of the miller.

1.   The adj. ſorgenfrei is used in allusion to the name of the king's palace, '*Sans souci.*' The miller was, perhaps, even more free from care than the king.

4.   In prose: in ɧeiſem unb faltem 𝔚etter.

6.   The verb aufbauen is very properly employed here, because the palace stands on high terraced ground.

12.   The king offers so much purchase-money that the miller will be enabled to build up another and much larger mill in some other spot.

15.   'My father laid his blessing on it.'

22.   Instead of ter ſtarre Ꮪinn we also find the compound ter Ꮪtarr-ſinn, 'obstinacy.'

27.   iɧ geb' miɧ trein, 'I submit to it'; synonymous phrases are, ſiɧ in etwaß ſɧiđen and fügen, ſiɧ mit etwaß zufrieten geben.

XXXII.

"A remarkable Prussian Hussar major [subsequently general], the famous Ziethen," is the expression of Carlyle in his *Frederick the Great*, book XII. ch. XIII.; "a rugged simple son of the moorlands ; nourished, body and soul, on orthodox frugal oatmeal (so to speak), with a large sprinkling of fire and iron thrown in! A man born poor, son of some poor squirelet in the Ruppin country—a big-headed, thick-lipped, decidedly ugly little man. And yet so beautiful in his ugliness: wise, resolute, true, with a dash of high uncomplaining sorrow in him. One of the best Hussar-captains ever built. By degrees King Frederick and he grew to be what we might call sworn friends." And in the account of Frederick's last years (1780—1785), book XXI. ch. VIII., Carlyle says, "Ziethen comes rarely, and falls asleep when he does," and in another passage (ch. V.) he relates the last meeting of the two friends when the king made Ziethen, then an old man of eighty-six, sit down while himself and all his suite remained standing.

The general tone and style of this ballad are eminently popular.

4.   Observe the construction er tɧ̨ȧt bieten, and comp. 5, 32.

6.   Ꮐinem ten 𝔓elʒ waſɧen is a popular expression, denoting 'to give some one a good drubbing.'

7.   𝔏eibɧuſaren, hussars of the guards.

9.   bláuen, or more commonly turɧbláuen, means 'to beat black and blue.' Comp. the phrase, Ꮐinen grün unb blau ſɧlagen.

10.   In the battle of Lowositz, Oct. 15, 1756, the Austrian general

Brown was beaten; the victory of Prague (where brave Schwerin fell) was obtained on May 6, 1757. The battle in the neighbourhood of Liegnitz was fought on Friday morning, the 15th of August, 1760 (Carlyle, book XX. ch. III.); the battle of Leuthen, as has already been mentioned, took place on the 5th of Dec., 1757. The arrangement is not strictly chronological.

13. The battle of Torgau (Nov. 3, 1760) was won by Ziethen alone, after the king had left the field of battle; see Carlyle's description, book XX. ch. V.

15 sq. ausfehren, 'to sweep clean.'

21. In prose we should say, es erwies sich keiner träge.

23. Ein kalter Schlag is a stroke of lightning which does not cause fire.

25. Der Friede is the peace of Hubertsburg, concluded on Feb. 21, 1763. In this peace Prussia obtained the undisputed possession of Silesia.

27. Der Schlachtgenosse, comrade in war.

29. Daun was a great *cunctator* in his method of warfare.

37. mir is the *dat. ethicus*, which is so common in German.

XXXIII.

Schill's name occupies a prominent place among the patriotic soldiers of the present century. Schill was born on the 6th of January, 1776, near Dresden, and entered, at the age of 16 years, into the same regiment of hussars, of which his father had been Oberstlieutenant. Schill distinguished · himself by his great bravery in the disastrous battle of Jena, in which he was severely wounded. He was then employed in various military commands, and charged with a mission to the Swedish court, after which he was stationed in Berlin. Towards the end of 1808, he resolved, though unsupported by the Prussian Government, to renew the war against the Corsican tyrant, then in the zenith of his power. On April 28, 1809, Schill left Berlin with a small force of 600 horsemen; on the night of the 29th he was reinforced by 300 volunteers. They marched to Wittenberg and Dessau, calling upon the people to rise against the French oppressors; but the French soldiers were already moving against Schill's scanty force. At Dodendorf, about a German mile from Magdeburg, Schill obtained a victory over the French troops sent against him; but his power was too insignificant to venture on besieging the fortress of Magdeburg, then in the hands of the French. He therefore proceeded to Stendal, and thence into Mecklenburg with a view to make for the coast where he hoped to find English ships. But the people did not rise anywhere, and Schill perceived that he was not strong enough to effect anything by himself. Meanwhile, Napoleon's brother, King Jerôme of Westphalia, had set a price of 10,000 francs on Schill's head, and a considerable French force was on its way against the daring adventurer. Schill now threw himself into the strong fortress of Stralsund, with a force which had gradually increased to the number of 1800 men. But instead of attacking the French before they could invest the town (comp. v. 36 sqq.), Schill imprudently resolved on standing a siege—a proceeding the more dangerous, because the king of Denmark (v. 36) had reinforced the French with an auxiliary force of 1500 men. The town was stormed by land and sea, and Schill's forces proved insufficient for a protracted defence. Though he and his soldiers performed marvels of valour, street after street was wrested from them, and at length Schill himself was killed. When his body was found and recognised, his head was cut off and sent to Cassel, and from thence to Leyden where it was long kept in spirits as a public show; in 1837 it was given up, and buried at Brunswick. Schill's trunk was buried in the cemetery of Stralsund, and his resting-place is now covered with a fitting monument. When Arndt wrote his poem, this monument had not yet been erected (comp. v. 54).

4. In prose we say nach etwas dürften.

5. im Schritt, keeping time (with the feet).

8. Franzmann, see note 22, 32.—erblaffen, a euphemistic term for sterben.

16. In prose we should say die übrigen machten lange Beine, i.e. ran away as fast as their legs would carry them. According to the ordinary rules of German pronunciation, lang would not rhyme with blank; but in the North of Germany, ng at the end of words often has the sound of nk.

17. Dömitz is a small fortress in Mecklenburg.

18. Schelmenfranzofen, 'the French rogues.' This compound was probably invented by Arndt. Comp. a song of 1870:

> Wenn all' die Schelmfranzofen
> Sind aus dem Land hinaus.

See R. Wülcker, *Fünfzig Feldpostbriefe eines Frankfurters* (Halle, 1876), p. 6.

20. Kiwi = Fr. *qui vit*, the cry of the French sentinels.

21. reisig is derived from reifen, which is originally identical with reiten; hence der reifige Zug means pretty much the same as the train of cavalry. Comp. v. 24.

26. Sich verliegen, to lie (in a place) with a bad result. See no. 26.

27. Charles XII., king of Sweden, was besieged in Stralsund by Prussia, Poland, and Denmark; there is a stone still shown in the fortifications of Stralsund with an inscription stating that it formed the usual resting-place for the king. *Sweriges konung Carl den XII hade här sit wanliga natläger da Stralsund belägrades af 3 kunungar från den 19 Octob. til den 22 Dec.* 1715.

28. The fortifications had been partially dismantled.

31. The horsemen feel their German blood stirring within them.

34. Bube is nowadays used like the E. *knave* (hence bübisch 'knavish'), but had, like this, once merely the meaning of 'boy.'

39. Observe the omission of the personal pronoun du after the verb. This would not be possible in correct prose, but is often noticed in homely everyday speech.

41. The trisyllabic form Stralefund is fully justified by the original name of the town, and moreover, the straits which divide Stralsund from the island of Rügen, are still called *Strela-Sund.*

49. The expression ohne Sang und Klang is proverbial, denoting the absence of all solemnity, or all the 'pomp and circumstance' of a funeral. Comp. the following lines.

51. Flintengruß (omitted in Grimm): 'military salute'; it is customary to fire a charge of musketry at a soldier's funeral.

55. Der jüngste Tag (i. e. *dies novissimus*), doomsday.

61 sq. This alludes to the time of the wars of 1813 and 1814, when Schill's memory at last received due honour, and his glorious, though rash, attempt was held up as an example of patriotism.

64. In prose we should, of course, be obliged to change the order of words.

XXXIV.

At the peace of Pressburg (26th Dec. 1805) Austria had been compelled to cede to Bavaria the rich province of the Tyrol. But the hearts of the Tyrolese remained faithful to the Habsburg dynasty, and the impolitic treatment they received at the hands of the Bavarian rulers, exasperated them so much that they rose into open rebellion. At the head of the insurgents was *Andreas Hofer,* „der Sandwirth im Passeyrthale," who enjoyed a great popularity among his compatriots, a brave and valorous man. Though at first successful against the French and the Bavarians, the unskilled peasants were finally overcome after the Austrian troops had been withdrawn. Andreas Hofer did, indeed, wonders of valour, and even obtained a splendid victory near the Iselberg (comp. v. 13); three times did he wrest the city of Innsbruck out of the hands of the enemy,—but in the end the French remained victorious. Hofer's hidingplace was betrayed by some greedy wretch, who wished to earn the prize set on his head ; the brave man was conducted to Mantua, and there shot by the order of Eugene, Viceroy of Italy. Hofer died with the courage of a hero and martyr, highly honoured by his people.

6. Observe the alliteration in Schmach und Schmerz.

9. Sandwirth, i.e. landlord of the tavern 'am Sand.'

10. ruhig is the adverb.

11. Death appeared to him as something quite insignificant. It is related that Hofer said shortly before his execution—Ade schnöde Welt ; so leicht kommt mir das Sterben vor, daß mir nicht einmal die Augen naß werden.

17. Waffenbrüder, companions in arms, the other Tyrolese who were prisoners in Mantua.

26. Even in fetters a free man.

30. For nit = nicht comp. 13, 23.

36. Comp. v. 8 sq.

39. Allhier is a somewhat pedantic, and in the present instance more impressive form than hier.

XXXV.

For an account of Blücher's great victory over the French under Marshal Macdonald in the battle of the Katzbach we refer to Kohlrausch, *The Year* 1813, published in the Pitt Press Series, pp. 36—39.

5. In prose it would be more usual to give this in the form of a conditional clause : wenn auch die Todeswunde brennt.

9. ringen (lit. 'to wrestle') is often used of the last struggles in the agonies of death.

10. In prose : in bangen Todesängsten.

14. wild expresses the strange excitement which has seized the trumpeter.

16. ein steinern Bild, a statue of stone.

19. The allusion is, of course, to the compound Donnerwetter. The phrase, Victoria (the signal of victory) wettert wie ein Donner in das Land (goes forth into the land with the sound of thunder) is anything but usual.

30. hielt's = hielt das.

XXXVI.

The 'fieldmarshal' celebrated in this spirited poem is Blücher, that prototype of a German warrior, whom his soldiers called Marschall Vorwärts, and whose praise has been recorded by Goethe in the pithy lines;

In Harren und Krieg,
Im Sturz und Sieg,
Bewußt und groß —
So riß er uns von Feinden los.

1. Was = warum, weßhalb.

2. im fliegenten Saus, 'in flying gallop.' Der Saus is not a very common noun, except in the proverbial phrase in Saus und Braus leben, to live recklessly.

4. schneitig from die Schneite, the edge of the sword.

6. wallen = im Winde flattern.

7. The verb greifen is very unusual, but easily understood. Old wine is better than fresh must, and possesses more flavour (called Blume in German, whence the expression blühen in the present line). Thus Blücher's matured experience is preferable to the rashness of younger soldiers.

9, 10. For the rhyme versank schwang, comp. 33, 16.

10. gen is a contraction of gegen. It is especially employed in a higher style.

12. Die Wälschen denotes here the French. "At various points on the frontiers of our race we find them affixing this name on the conterminous Romance-speaking people. This is the most probable account of the names *Wallachia*, the *Walloons* in Belgium, and the Canton *Wallis* in Switzerland. On this principle we call the Romanised Britons, and the Germans called the Italians, by the same name—Welsh." Earle, *The Philology of the English Tongue*, ed. 2, p. 23. Blücher was one of the few who maintained the honour of the Prussian arms after the disastrous battle of Jena.

14. The interjection hei is quite appropriate to the spirited and popular style of this poem. It is very common in the ancient poem of the Nibelunge.—Der weiße Jüngling, the youth with white hair. Though old in years Blücher had preserved all the spring and elasticity of youth. (Comp. also Kohlrausch p. 52, 7.)—in'n = in den would be inadmissible in prose or ordinary poetry; it is a shortening permitted by the popular style.

15. Comp. the similar expressions in 32, 15 sq.

17. Einen Strauß halten, 'to fight a battle.' For the word Strauß see note on 4, 52.

19. The adj. hasig (from Hase) is very uncommon. Grimm quotes only the present instance of the word. 'They ran away like hares.' Comp. v. 27.

22. The verb lehren is either construed with two accusatives (einen

etwas lehren), or the person who is taught something may be put in the dative (as we have it here). In the passive we may either say, ich werde etwas gelehrt, or mir wird etwas gelehrt. Compare with this the Latin construction of *docere.*

24. Ohnehosen is a translation of the term *Sansculottes,* originally applied to the democratic party in the French revolution, and here to the whole French army.

25. The original form of the name is Wartenburg. For the battle of Wartenburg, we refer to Kohlrausch p. 52 sq.

31. sicher, so as not to rise again.

35. This poem was written about the close of 1813, before Blücher had crossed the Rhine, and advanced into France.

XXXVII.

For the formation and history of Lützow's corps we may refer to Kohlrausch, *The Year* 1813, p. 27, with our notes.

1. vom Walde=vom W. her; the bold riders being conceived as advancing from the side of the wood. As we are not supposed to be aware of the exact description of the sight exciting our attention, the neuter pronoun es is employed in the following lines.

4. For darein see n. on 3, 31.

6. die schwarzen Gesellen, 'the black lads.'

9. In prose: von einem Berg zum andern.

12. fränkisch=französisch. In its proper application, this adj. may be used (1) of the ancient tribe of the Franks who conquered Gaul in the fifth century; (2) of the modern province of Franconia, on the upper Maine.—Schergen is here contemptuously used of the soldiers of Napoleon. Comp. Henkersblut v. 37.

16. Der Wütrich (a term often applied to a furious tyrant) should of course be understood of Napoleon.—meinte is here identical with wähnte, inasmuch as his hope was without foundation.

17. The riders dash up to the brink of the river like far-shining tempest and lightning.

24. Wildherzig is not a very usual adjective, though easily understood. Sanders quotes another instance of it from Voss's translation of Homer: So wildherzig ist Keiner, daß Nichts ihn bändigen könnte.

30. winseln is properly used of dogs, though it is also employed in a wider sense. Luther has it even of birds: Ich winselte wie ein Kranich und Schwalbe. Jes. xxxviii. 14.

38. We should notice the idiomatic use of the past participle

instead of the imperative.   See our note on Goethe's *Hermann and Dorothea* 1, 174.

39. tagen corresponds to *dawn* both in etymology and in meaning; here the new morning which begins to dawn should be understood metaphorically of liberty.

41. nachfagen means 'to repeat after some one': comp. Goethe as quoted by Sanders: Dergleichen Redensarten fagen fich nach, pflanzen fich fort.

XXXVIII.

For the events which form the groundwork of this poem, we may be allowed to refer to the account given by Kohlrausch as edited in the Pitt Press Series (*The Year* 1813), p. 26 sq.   For Scharnhorst's bravery in the battle of Lützen (or Grossgörschen) on May 2, 1813, see *ibid.* p. 17.

1. The 'dance of war' is a frequent expression for war itself. Comp. Schiller:

> Theures Weib, geh', hol' die Todestanze,
> Laßt mich fort zum wilden Kriegestanze.

2. There is a certain ambiguity in the expression of the poet, inasmuch as it is possible to take both Heldenlanze and General as subject. According to the first explanation, brach would be intransitive (= 'was broken') and General would be the apposition: 'there broke your fairest lance, your general.'   We should, however, prefer another explanation, according to which the order of words would be euer General brach (trans.) die schönste Heldenlanze, in the sense of 'he fought most bravely.' Eine Lanze brechen is a phrase derived from tournaments, quite equivalent to the E. *to break a lance* for someone.—The compound Heldenlanze is not registered in Grimm.

5. Freiheitswaffen are arms taken up in defence of liberty—a compound not registered in Grimm.

7. The omission of the personal pronoun du after raffst is poetical and colloquial.   In the same manner, we should supply ich in the next line in prose: noch blutend will ich euch dienen.   Comp. v. 15.

10. werben is here used in the general sense of *suing* for some one's friendship and alliance.

11. Ist's beschlossen = wenn es (einmal so) beschlossen ist (decreed by fate).

12. Schwerin (Kurt Christoph, Graf von), one of the generals of Frederick II. of Prussia, fell in the battle of Prague, May 6, 1757.

14. This is an allusion to the fate which is said to have befallen St Nepomuk, the confessor of the queen of Wenceslaus, king of Bohemia; having refused to betray the queen's confessions to her jealous husband,

he is said to have been thrown from the bridge into the river *Moldau*, on which Prague is situated. Nepomuk is now considered the patron saint of Prague.

19. Getümmel, 'stir, turmoil.'

22. The sense is evidently intended to be zu tem Rathe ter alten Deutschen.

23. Staat is used in the same way as *state* in poetical English. Charlemagne is conceived as presiding in state over the heavenly council of genuine old Germany.

26. Zeitung = Nachricht, comp. *tidings*.

29. Sühnungswunten is a word probably coined by our poet; it would be more usual to say tie Sühnwunte.

33. The common alliance of all German tribes against Napoleon should strive to transform Scharnhorst's word into actual truth and deed. The present poem was composed anterior to the battle of Leipzig, in which the liberty of Germany was finally asserted against the French.

34. Scharnhorst had been very active in the re-organisation of the Prussian army, which formed the surest guarantee of victory.

37. Bergesforst, a compound easily understood, is not registered in Grimm.

42. Does the poet mean to connect the name of Scharnhorst with the verb horsten and the noun Aar, which is often used in poetry as a synonym of Adler? The idea is certainly very far-fetched.

45. tem Volke is dativus commodi, in the sense of für tas Volk.

XXXIX.

A pithy little poem expressive of Blücher's bluntness and quickness of decision. Many of the leaders of the allied armies hesitated whether it would be advisable to cross the Rhine and pursue the flying enemy into France, but Blücher's vote carried the day, and he was the first to cross, in the night of new year's day, 1814.

5. A short command instead of gebt mir tie Generalfarte her!

7. Dahier may be compared with allhier, 34, 39.

8. Den Finger trauf, here and line 10, contains an admonition to mark the enemy's position by pointing out the place in the map.

13. It would be more usual to add ta before the relative sentence.

XL.

We have thought fit to include in our collection this fine poem, which attained to such great celebrity in the late memorable war. It was written thirty years before 1870, but became famous in that year, when the enthusiasm of the whole German nation was excited to its greatest pitch. The poet himself had long been dead when his song resounded from one end of Germany to the other.

2. 𝔚𝔬𝔤𝔢𝔫𝔭𝔯𝔞𝔩𝔩, the dash of waves (against a rocky shore).

7. 𝔷𝔲𝔠𝔨𝔢𝔫 is the expression used of the electric spark which thrills through the body. See 26, 82.

10. 𝔐𝔞𝔯𝔨 is the old appellation of the boundary district, like the English *marches*. Hence 𝔐𝔞𝔯𝔨𝔤𝔯𝔞𝔣, marquis.

13. 𝔇𝔞𝔰 𝔅𝔩𝔞𝔲𝔢𝔫 𝔡𝔢𝔰 𝔥𝔦𝔪𝔪𝔢𝔩𝔰 is a poetical expression instead of the ordinary 𝔡𝔢𝔯 𝔟𝔩𝔞𝔲𝔢 𝔥𝔦𝔪𝔪𝔢𝔩.

14. 𝔚𝔬 = 𝔳𝔬𝔫 𝔴𝔬𝔥𝔢𝔯.

20. 𝔚𝔞̈𝔩𝔰𝔠𝔥𝔢𝔯: comp. 36, 12.—These lines are addressed to the river Rhine, which the French poet Alfred de Musset had claimed as belonging to his nation by right of conquest:

> Nous l'avons eu, votre Rhin allemand—
> Son sein porte une plaie ouverte,
> Du jour où Condé triomphant
> A déchiré sa robe verte.
> Où le père a passé, passera bien l'enfant.

31. rinnt = 'runs' in its original meaning. In modern German rinnen is to trickle, to flow gently.

XLI.

By the battles fought around Metz on the 14th, 16th, and 18th of August, 1870 (commonly called the battle of Gravelotte, where the last fight on the 18th took place), the French under *Bazaine* were beaten and thrown back into the fortress of *Metz*.

4. The epithet 𝔪𝔞̈𝔫𝔫𝔢𝔯𝔪𝔬𝔯𝔱𝔢𝔫𝔡 is Homeric; in Homer it is employed of the god of war, Ares.

9. The smoke of the repeated discharges of artillery hovered like a thick fog over the field of battle.

10. 𝔲̈𝔟𝔢𝔯𝔰𝔞𝔱𝔱, more than sated, surfeited. The genitive after 𝔰𝔞𝔱𝔱 is poetical; in prose the prepositions 𝔳𝔬𝔫 and 𝔪𝔦𝔱 are more commonly used with this adj.

13. Death is represented as a mere skeleton of bones, without flesh and skin.

15. 𝔇𝔞𝔰 𝔊𝔢𝔰𝔱𝔦𝔯𝔫 𝔡𝔢𝔰 𝔗𝔞𝔤𝔢𝔰 is the sun.

16. 𝔷𝔲𝔯 𝔯𝔲̈𝔰𝔱𝔢 𝔤𝔢𝔥𝔢𝔫 is an archaic and poetical expression identical in sense with the ordinary 𝔷𝔲𝔯 𝔯𝔲𝔥𝔢 or 𝔷𝔲𝔯 𝔯𝔞𝔰𝔱 𝔤𝔢𝔥𝔢𝔫.—𝔇𝔦𝔢 𝔣𝔦𝔯𝔫𝔢 𝔡𝔢𝔯 𝔅𝔢𝔯𝔤𝔢, the tops of the mountains. Originally 𝔣𝔦𝔯𝔫 or 𝔣𝔦𝔯𝔫𝔢 denotes the never-melting snow of the highest mountains in the Alps.

19. The preposition an expresses approximate estimation; 'about.'

21. For the adj. unabſehbar see our note on Goethe's *Hermann and Dorothea*, I, 107.

22. 'A gaping sepulchre of nations.'

23. Sternenzelt is an expression like Himmelszelt, 8, 12.

29. The poet is, as it were, present on the field of battle, amid the heaps of slain.—Ihr treuen Todten, see Aue § 175, 3.

42 sq. The allusion is to Prometheus, who was chained to the Caucasus by the command of Jupiter.

44. baar, with the genitive, is poetical, in the sense of 'deprived,' beraubt.

45. It is more common to use the reflective of this verb, ſich aufbäumend.

46. The eagle is well known as the armorial emblem of Germany. Prometheus' liver was torn and devoured by an eagle, while he himself was chained to the rock.

51. In prose: in ununterbrochenem Zuge.

55. Observe the heavy sound of the compound, Sturmmarſchtritt, which resembles the heavy tramp of an army marching in time.

XLII.

King William of Prussia, born on 22nd March, 1797, succeeded his brother, Frederick William IV., on 2nd Jan., 1861, and was proclaimed German Emperor on 18th Jan., 1871. This proclamation took place at Versailles, in the palace erected by Louis XIV.

2. This line and the one preceding it are an imitation of the opening lines of Bürger's famous Lied vom braven Manne:

Hoch klingt das Lied vom braven Mann,
Wie Orgelton und Glockenklang.

9. See no. 14 in the present collection, together with our introductory note. The expression Rabenbrut, in v. 11, is likewise explained by this reference.

16. der Einheit Eiche, the oak, emblem of German strength and unity.

26. The usual form is hochgemuth.

27. todbereit = bereit zum Tode.

33—40 have been most obligingly rewritten by the poet, expressly for the present collection. What he had in 1871 expressed in the form of a wish has meanwhile, to a certain degree, been fulfilled, and the auspicious reign of the first German Emperor of the House of Hohenzollern has already been productive of a large amount of the blessings enumerated in these lines!

NOTES ON THE AUTHORS OF THE POEMS UNITED
IN THE PRESENT COLLECTION.

ARNDT (Ernst Moritz), born at Schoritz in the Isle of Rügen, 26th Dec. 1769, one of the foremost patriots in the wars of 1813 and 1814, subsequently professor at the University of Bonn, where he died 29th Jan. 1860. [33, 36.]

BAUR (Karl), born at Darmstädt in 1788, professor at the College of his native town. [4.]

BESSER (Hermann), born at Zeitz in 1807, lives at Potsdam in the position of *Regierungs-Assessor*. [30.]

CHAMISSO (Adalbert von), by birth a Frenchman, whose original name was Louis Charles Adelaide de Chamisso de Boncourt, born in the castle of Boncourt in Champagne, 27th Jan. 1781, was driven out of his native country by the revolution and became a thorough German. Died at Berlin, 21st Aug. 1838. [12.]

CURTMANN (Wilhelm Jacob), born at Alsfeld in Hessia, 3rd March, 1802, headmaster at Worms. [31.]

. DOHM (E.), author of various poems, lives in Berlin as editor of the *Kladderadatsch* (the German *Punch*). [41.]

ELZE (Karl), one of the foremost Shakespeare-critics in Germany, formerly at Dessau, now professor of English literature at the University of Halle. [42.]

FONTANE (Theodor), born at Neu-Ruppin, 30th Dec. 1819, studied Natural Philosophy at Berlin, then lived at Leipzig and Dresden, spent four years in London, and returned to Berlin in 1859, where he lives now as secretary to the Academy. [32.]

FREILIGRATH (Ferdinand), born at Detmold, 17th June, 1810, originally merchant, lived in London 1851—1868, when he returned to Germany. He died at Cannstatt 18th March 1876. [28.]

GRÜN (Anastasius) is the *nom de plume* of the Austrian Count Anton Alexander Maria Auersperg, born at Laibach in Krain 11th April 1806, died at Graz 12th Sept. 1876. [22.]

GÜNTHER (Karl Friedrich), born at Altenburg in 1807. He holds the dignity of *Diaconus* in his native town. [26.]

HAGENBACH (Karl Rudolf), born at Basle 4th May 1801, professor of theology at the University of his native town. [23, 24.]

KERNER (Justinus), born at Ludwigsburg, 18th Sept. 1786, physician at Weinsberg, where he died 22nd Feb. 1862. [18, 21.]

KOPISCH (August), born at Breslau 26th May 1799, lived as painter at Berlin, where he died 6th Feb. 1853. [3, 39.]

KÖRNER (Theodor), born at Dresden 31st Sept. 1791, joined

Lützow's corps, and fell in a skirmish near Gadebusch in Mecklenburg, 26th August 1813. [37.]

MENZEL (Wolfgang), born at Waldenburg in Silesia 21st June 1798, died at Stuttgart 23rd April 1873. [19.]

MINDING (Julius), born at Breslau 8th Nov. 1808, studied medicine, and terminated his life by committing suicide, in New York, 7th Sept. 1850. [27.]

MOSEN (Julius), born in Voigtland (Saxony) 8th July 1803, was first solicitor at Dresden, and accepted in 1844 the appointment of manager to the Grand-Ducal Theatre at Oldenburg, from which position he retired in 1848, on account of impaired health. He died 10th Oct. 1867. [34, 35.]

MÜHLER (Heinrich von), born 4th Nov. 1812, sometime Prussian minister of Instruction, died at Potsdam in 1874. [9.]

PLATEN (August, Graf von P.-Hallermünde), born at Ansbach, 24th Oct. 1796, died at Syracuse, 5th Dec. 1835. [1, 6, 10, 25.]

RÜCKERT (Friedrich), born at Schweinfurt, 16th May 1789, professor at Erlangen (1826) and subsequently at Berlin (1841), concluded his life on his estate near Coburg, 31st Jan. 1866. [14.]

SCHENKENDORF (Max von), born at Tilsit 11th Dec. 1783, died at Coblenz on the Rhine 1817, on his birthday. [38.]

SCHILLER (Friedrich von), born at Marbach, 10th Nov. 1759, died at Weimar, 9th May 1805. [17.]

SCHNECKENBURGER (Max), born at Thalheim near Tuttlingen in the kingdom of Würtemberg, 27th Feb. 1819, owner of an ironfoundry at Burgdorf in Switzerland, where he died in the flower of his age in 1849. [40.]

SCHWAB (Gustav), born at Stuttgart, 19th June 1792, professor of classical literature at the College of his native town until 1837, then pastor at Gomaringen near Tübingen, 1841 pastor at St Leonard's Church, Stuttgart, died there 3rd Nov. 1850. [11.]

SIMROCK (Karl), born at Bonn 28th Aug. 1802, professor of German literature at the University of Bonn, where he died 18th July 1876. [2.]

STOLTERFOTH (Adelheid von), baroness of Zwierlein, born at Eisenach 11th Sept. 1800, died in 1875. [7.]

UHLAND (Johann Ludwig), born at Tübingen 26th April 1787, died there 13th Nov. 1862. [5, 13, 15, 20.]

VOGL (Johann Nepomuck), born at Vienna in 1802, died there 16th Nov. 1866. [8.]

ZIMMERMANN (B. F. Wilhelm), born at Stuttgart 2nd Jan. 1807, professor at the College of his native town. [16.]

CAMBRIDGE: PRINTED BY C. J. CLAY, M.A. AT THE UNIVERSITY PRESS.

UNIVERSITY PRESS, CAMBRIDGE.
May, 1880.

PUBLICATIONS OF
The Cambridge University Press.

___

THE HOLY SCRIPTURES, &c.

The Cambridge Paragraph Bible of the Authorized English
Version, with the Text revised by a Collation of its Early and
other Principal Editions, the Use of the Italic Type made uniform,
the Marginal References remodelled, and a Critical Introduction
prefixed, by the Rev. F. H. SCRIVENER, M.A., LL.D., one of the
Revisers of the Authorized Version. Crown Quarto, cloth gilt, 21*s*.

THE STUDENT'S EDITION of the above, on *good writing paper*, with
one column of print and wide margin to each page for MS. notes.
Two Vols. Crown Quarto, cloth, gilt, 31*s*. 6*d*.

The Lectionary Bible, with Apocrypha, divided into Sec-
tions adapted to the Calendar and Tables of Lessons of 1871.
Crown Octavo, cloth, 3*s*. 6*d*.

Breviarium ad usum insignis Ecclesiae Sarum. Fasciculus II.
In quo continentur PSALTERIUM, cum ordinario Officii totius
hebdomadae juxta Horas Canonicas, et proprio Completorii,
LITANIA, COMMUNE SANCTORUM, ORDINARIUM MISSAE CUM
CANONE ET XIII MISSIS, &c. &c. juxta Editionem maximam
pro CLAUDIO CHEVALLON et FRANCISCO REGNAULT A. D.
MDXXXI. in Alma Parisiorum Academia impressam : labore ac
studio FRANCISCI PROCTER, A.M., et CHRISTOPHORI WORDS-
WORTH, A.M. Demy 8vo., cloth, 12*s*.

The Pointed Prayer Book, being the Book of Common
Prayer with the Psalter or Psalms of David, pointed as they are
to be sung or said in Churches. Embossed cloth, Royal 24mo, 2*s*.

The same in square 32mo, cloth, 6*d*.

The Cambridge Psalter, for the use of Choirs and Organists.
Specially adapted for Congregations in which the "Cambridge
Pointed Prayer Book" is used. Demy 8vo. cloth, 3*s*. 6*d*. Cloth
limp cut flush, 2*s*. 6*d*.

The Paragraph Psalter, arranged for the use of Choirs by
BROOKE FOSS WESTCOTT, D D., Canon of Peterborough, and
Regius Professor of Divinity, Cambridge. Fcp. 4to. 5*s*.

Greek and English Testament, in parallel columns on the
same page. Edited by J. SCHOLEFIELD, M.A. late Regius Professor of Greek in the University. *New Edition, with the marginal
references as arranged and revised by* DR SCRIVENER. Cloth, red
edges. 7*s*. 6*d*. _____

London: Cambridge Warehouse, 17 *Paternoster Row.*

3000
14/5/80

Greek and English Testament. THE STUDENT'S EDITION of the above on *large writing paper*. 4to. cloth. 12s.

Greek Testament, ex editione Stephani tertia, 1550. Small Octavo. 3s. 6d.

The Gospel according to St Matthew in Anglo-Saxon and Northumbrian Versions, synoptically arranged: with Collations of the best Manuscripts. By J. M. KEMBLE, M.A. and Archdeacon HARDWICK. Demy Quarto. 10s.

The Gospel according to St Mark in Anglo-Saxon and Northumbrian Versions, synoptically arranged, with Collations exhibiting all the Readings of all the MSS. Edited by the Rev. Professor SKEAT, M.A. Demy Quarto. 10s.

The Gospel according to St Luke, uniform with the preceding, edited by the Rev. Professor SKEAT. Demy Quarto. 10s.

The Gospel according to St John, uniform with the preceding, edited by the Rev. Professor SKEAT. Demy Quarto. 10s.

The Missing Fragment of the Latin Translation of the Fourth Book of Ezra, discovered, and edited with an Introduction and Notes, and a facsimile of the MS., by R. L. BENSLY, M.A., Fellow of Gonville and Caius College. Cloth, 10s.

THEOLOGY—(ANCIENT).

Sayings of the Jewish Fathers, comprising Pirqe Aboth and Pereq R. Meir in Hebrew and English, with Critical and Illustrative Notes; and specimen pages of the Cambridge University Manuscript of the Mishnah 'Jerushalmith'. By C. TAYLOR, M.A., Fellow and Divinity Lecturer of St John's College. Demy Octavo. 10s.

Theodore of Mopsuestia's Commentary on the Minor Epistles of S. Paul. The Latin Version with the Greek Fragments, edited from the MSS. with Notes and an Introduction, by H. B. SWETE, B.D , Rector of Ashdon, Essex, and late Fellow of Gonville and Caius College, Cambridge. In two Volumes. Vol. I., containing the Introduction, and the Commentary upon Galatians—Colossians. Demy Octavo. 12s.

Sancti Irenæi Episcopi Lugdunensis libros quinque adversus Hæreses, versione Latina cum Codicibus Claromontano ac Arundeliano denuo collata, præmissa de placitis Gnosticorum prolusione, fragmenta necnon Græce, Syriace, Armeniace, commentatione perpetua et indicibus variis edidit W. WIGAN HARVEY, S.T.B. Collegii Regalis olim Socius. 2 Vols. Demy Octavo. 18s.

M. Minucii Felicis Octavius. The text newly revised from the original MS. with an English Commentary, Analysis, Introduction, and Copious Indices. Edited by H. A. HOLDEN, LL.D. Head Master of Ipswich School, late Fellow of Trinity College, Cambridge. Crown Octavo. 7s. 6d.

Theophili Episcopi Antiochensis Libri Tres ad Autolycum. Edidit, Prolegomenis Versione Notulis Indicibus instruxit GULIELMUS GILSON HUMPHRY, S.T.B. Post Octavo. 5s.

Theophylacti in Evangelium S. Matthæi Commentarius. Edited by W. G. HUMPHRY, B.D. Demy Octavo. 7s. 6d.

Tertullianus de Corona Militis, de Spectaculis, de Idololatria, with Analysis and English Notes, by GEORGE CURREY, D.D. Master of the Charter House. Crown Octavo. 5s.

THEOLOGY—(ENGLISH).

Works of Isaac Barrow, compared with the original MSS., enlarged with Materials hitherto unpublished. A new Edition, by A. NAPIER, M.A. of Trinity College, Vicar of Holkham, Norfolk. Nine Vols. Demy Octavo. £3. 3s.

Treatise of the Pope's Supremacy, and a Discourse concerning the Unity of the Church, by ISAAC BARROW. Demy Octavo. 7s. 6d.

Pearson's Exposition of the Creed, edited by TEMPLE CHEVALLIER, B.D., late Professor of Mathematics in the University of Durham, and Fellow and Tutor of St Catharine's College, Cambridge. Second Edition. Demy Octavo. 7s. 6d.

An Analysis of the Exposition of the Creed, written by the Right Rev. Father in God, JOHN PEARSON, D.D., late Lord Bishop of Chester. Compiled for the use of the Students of Bishop's College, Calcutta, by W. H. MILL, D.D. late Regius Professor of Hebrew in the University of Cambridge. Demy Octavo, cloth. 5s.

Wheatly on the Common Prayer, edited by G. E. CORRIE, D.D. Master of Jesus College, Examining Chaplain to the late Lord Bishop of Ely. Demy Octavo. 7s. 6d.

The Homilies, with Various Readings, and the Quotations from the Fathers given at length in the Original Languages. Edited by G. E. CORRIE, D.D. Master of Jesus College. Demy Octavo. 7s. 6d.

Two Forms of Prayer of the time of Queen Elizabeth. Now First Reprinted. Demy Octavo. 6d.

Select Discourses, by JOHN SMITH, late Fellow of Queens' College, Cambridge. Edited by H. G. WILLIAMS, B.D. late Professor of Arabic. Royal Octavo. 7s. 6d.

Cæsar Morgan's Investigation of the Trinity of Plato, and of Philo Judæus, and of the effects which an attachment to their writings had upon the principles and reasonings of the Fathers of the Christian Church. Revised by H. A. HOLDEN, LL.D. Head Master of Ipswich School, late Fellow oᶠ Trinity College, Cambridge. Crown Octavo. 4s.

De Obligatione Conscientiæ Prælectiones decem Oxonii in Schola Theologica habitæ a ROBERTO SANDERSON, SS. Theologiæ ibidem Professore Regio. With English Notes, including an abridged Translation, by W. WHEWELL, D.D. late Master of Trinity College. Demy Octavo. 7s. 6d.

Archbishop Usher's Answer to a Jesuit, with other Tracts on Popery. Edited by J. SCHOLEFIELD, M.A. late Regius Professor of Greek in the University. Demy Octavo. 7s. 6d.

Wilson's Illustration of the Method of explaining the New Testament, by the early opinions of Jews and Christians concerning Christ. Edited by T. TURTON, D.D. late Lord Bishop of Ely. Demy Octavo. 5s.

Lectures on Divinity delivered in the University of Cambridge. By JOHN HEY, D.D. Third Edition, by T. TURTON, D.D. late Lord Bishop of Ely. 2 vols. Demy Octavo. 15s.

GREEK AND LATIN CLASSICS, &c.

(*See also* pp. 12, 13.)

The Agamemnon of Aeschylus. With a translation in English Rhythm, and Notes Critical and Explanatory. By BENJAMIN HALL KENNEDY, D.D., Regius Professor of Greek. Crown 8vo. 6s.

The Theætetus of Plato by the same Editor. [*In the Press.*

P. Vergili Maronis Opera, cum Prolegomenis et Commentario Critico pro Syndicis Preli Academici edidit BENJAMIN HALL KENNEDY, S.T.P., Graecae Linguae Professor Regius. Cloth, extra fcp. 8vo, red edges, price 5s.

Select Private Orations of Demosthenes with Introductions and English Notes, by F. A. PALEY, M.A., Editor of Aeschylus, etc. and J. E. SANDYS, M.A., Fellow and Tutor of St John's College, and Public Orator in the University of Cambridge.
Part I. containing Contra Phormionem, Lacritum, Pantaenetum, Boeotum de Nomine, Boeotum de Dote, Dionysodorum. Crown Octavo, cloth. 6s.
Part II. containing Pro Phormione, Contra Stephanum I. II.; Nicostratum, Cononem, Calliclem. Crown Octavo, cloth. 7s. 6d.

The Bacchae of Euripides, with Introduction, Critical Notes, and Archæological Illustrations, by J. E. SANDYS, M.A., Fellow and Tutor of St John's College, and Public Orator. [*Nearly ready.*

M. T. Ciceronis de Natura Deorum Libri Tres, with Introduction and Commentary by JOSEPH B MAYOR, M.A., Professor of Classical Literature at King's College, London, together with a new collation of several of the English MSS. by J. H. SWAINSON, M.A., formerly Fellow of Trinity College, Cambridge. [*Nearly ready.*

M. T. Ciceronis de Officiis Libri Tres with Marginal Analysis, an English Commentary, and Indices. Third Edition, revised, with numerous additions, by H. A. HOLDEN, LL.D., Head Master of Ipswich School. Crown Octavo, cloth. 9s.

M. T. Ciceronis pro Cn. Plancio oratio by the same Editor.
[*In the Press.*

Plato's Phædo, literally translated, by the late E. M. COPE, Fellow of Trinity College, Cambridge. Demy Octavo. 5s.

Aristotle. The Rhetoric. With a Commentary by the late E. M. COPE, Fellow of Trinity College, Cambridge, revised and edited by J. E. SANDYS, M.A., Fellow and Tutor of St John's College, and Public Orator. 3 Vols. Demy 8vo. £1 11s. 6d.

ΠΕΡΙ ΔΙΚΑΙΟΣΥΝΗΣ. The Fifth Book of the Nicomachean Ethics of Aristotle. Edited by HENRY JACKSON, M.A., Fellow of Trinity College, Cambridge. Demy 8vo, cloth. 6s.

Pindar. Olympian and Pythian Odes. With Notes Explanatory and Critical, Introductions and Introductory Essays. Edited by C. A. M. FENNELL, M.A., late Fellow of Jesus College. Crown 8vo. cloth. 9s.

The Isthmian and Nemean Odes by the same Editor.
[*Preparing.*

London: Cambridge Warehouse, 17 *Paternoster Row.*

SANSKRIT AND ARABIC.

Nalopākhyānam, or, The Tale of Nala; containing the San-skrit Text in Roman Characters, followed by a Vocabulary and a sketch of Sanskrit Grammar. By the Rev. THOMAS JARRETT, M.A., Regius Professor of Hebrew. Demy Octavo. 10s.

The Poems of Beha ed din Zoheir of Egypt. With a Metrical Translation, Notes and Introduction, by E. H. PALMER, M.A., Lord Almoner's Professor of Arabic in the University of Cambridge. 3 vols. Crown Quarto. Vol. II. The ENGLISH TRANSLATION. Paper cover, 10s. 6d. Cloth extra, 15s. [Vol. I. The ARABIC TEXT is already published.]

MATHEMATICS, PHYSICAL SCIENCE, &c.

A Treatise on Natural Philosophy. Volume I. Part I. By Sir W. THOMSON, LL.D., D.C.L., F.R.S., Professor of Natural Philosophy in the University of Glasgow, and P. G. TAIT, M.A., Professor of Natural Philosophy in the University of Edinburgh. Demy 8vo. cloth, 16s.

Elements of Natural Philosophy. By Professors Sir W. THOMSON and P. G. TAIT. Part I. *Second Edition*. 8vo. cloth, 9s.

An Elementary Treatise on Quaternions. By P. G. TAIT, M.A., Professor of Natural Philosophy in the University of Edinburgh. *Second Edition.* Demy 8vo. 14s.

A Treatise on the Theory of Determinants and their Ap-plications in Analysis and Geometry. By ROBERT FORSYTH SCOTT. M.A., of Lincoln's Inn; Fellow of St John's College, Cambridge. Demy 8vo. 12s.

Counterpoint. A practical course of study. By Professor G. A. MACFARREN, Mus. Doc. Second Edition, revised. Demy 4to. cloth. 7s. 6d.

The Analytical Theory of Heat. By JOSEPH FOURIER. Translated, with Notes, by A. FREEMAN, M.A., Fellow of St John's College, Cambridge. Demy 8vo. 16s.

Mathematical and Physical Papers. By ·GEORGE GABRIEL STOKES, M.A., D.C.L., LL.D., F.R.S., Fellow of Pembroke College and Lucasian Professor of Mathematics. Reprinted from the Original Journals and Transactions, with additional Notes by the Author. Vol. I.   [*Nearly ready.*]

London : Cambridge Warehouse, 17 Paternoster Row.

The Electrical Researches of the Honourable Henry Caven-dish, F.R.S. Written between 1771 and 1781, Edited from the original manuscripts in the possession of the Duke of Devonshire, K.G., by J. CLERK MAXWELL, F.R.S. Demy 8vo. cloth, 18s.

Hydrodynamics, a Treatise on the Mathematical Theory of Fluid Motion, by HORACE LAMB, M.A., formerly Fellow of Trinity College, Cambridge; Professor of Mathematics in the University of Adelaide. Demy 8vo. cloth, 12s.

The Mathematical Works of Isaac Barrow, D.D. Edited by W. WHEWELL, D.D. Demy Octavo. 7s. 6d.

Illustrations of Comparative Anatomy, Vertebrate and In-vertebrate, for the Use of Students in the Museum of Zoology and Comparative Anatomy. Second Edition. Demy 8vo. cloth, 2s. 6d.

A Catalogue of Australian Fossils (including Tasmania and the Island of Timor), by R. ETHERIDGE, Jun., F.G.S., Acting Palæontologist, H.M. Geol. Survey of Scotland. Demy 8vo. 10s.6d.

A Synopsis of the Classification of the British Palæozoic Rocks, by the Rev. ADAM SEDGWICK, M.A., F.R.S., with a systematic description of the British Palæozoic Fossils in the Geological Museum of the University of Cambridge, by FREDERICK MᶜCOY, F.G.S. One vol., Royal Quarto, cloth, Plates, £1. 1s.

A Catalogue of the Collection of Cambrian and Silurian Fossils contained in the Geological Museum of the University of Cambridge, by J. W. SALTER, F.G.S. With a Preface by the Rev. ADAM SEDGWICK, F.R.S. With a Portrait of PROFESSOR SEDGWICK. Royal Quarto, cloth, 7s. 6d.

Catalogue of Osteological Specimens contained in the Ana-tomical Museum of the University of Cambridge. Demy 8vo. 2s. 6d.

Astronomical Observations made at the Observatory of Cam-bridge by the Rev. JAMES CHALLIS, M.A., F.R.S., F.R.A.S., Plumian Professor of Astronomy from 1846 to 1860.

Astronomical Observations from 1861 to 1865. Vol. XXI. Royal Quarto, cloth, 15s.

LAW.

A Selection of the State Trials. By J. W. WILLIS-BUND, M.A., LL.B., Barrister-at-Law, Professor of Constitutional Law and His-tory, University College, London. Vol. I. Trials for Treason (1327—1660). Crown 8vo., cloth. 18s. Vol. II. [*In the Press.*

London: Cambridge Warehouse, 17 Paternoster Row.

The Fragments of the Perpetual Edict of Salvius Julianus, Collected, Arranged, and Annotated by BRYAN WALKER, MA., LL.D., Law Lecturer of St John's College, and late Fellow of Corpus Christi College, Cambridge. Crown 8vo., cloth. *Price 6s.*

The Commentaries of Gaius and Rules of Ulpian. (*New Edition.*) Translated and Annotated, by J. T. ABDY, LL.D., late Regius Professor of Laws, and BRYAN WALKER, M.A., LL.D., Law Lecturer of St John's College. Crown Octavo, 16s.

The Institutes of Justinian, translated with Notes by J. T. ABDY, LL.D., and BRYAN WALKER, M.A., LLD., St John's College, Cambridge. Crown Octavo, 16s.

Selected Titles from the Digest, annotated by BRYAN WALKER, M.A., LL.D. Part I. Mandati vel Contra. Digest xvii. 1. Crown Octavo, 5s.

Part II. **De Adquirendo rerum dominio,** and **De Adquirenda** vel amittenda Possessione, Digest XLI. 1 and 2. Crown 8vo. 6s.

Grotius de Jure Belli et Pacis, with the Notes of Barbeyrac and others; accompanied by an abridged Translation of the Text, by W. WHEWELL, D.D. late Master of Trinity College. 3 Vols. Demy Octavo, 12s. The translation separate, 6s.

HISTORICAL WORKS.

Life and Times of Stein, or Germany and Prussia in the Napoleonic Age, by J. R. SEELEY, M.A., Regius Professor of Modern History in the University of Cambridge. With Portraits and Maps. 3 vols. Demy 8vo. 48s.

Scholae Academicae: some Account of the Studies at the English Universities in the Eighteenth Century. By CHRISTOPHER WORDSWORTH, M.A., Fellow of Peterhouse; Author of "Social Life at the English Universities in the Eighteenth Century." Demy Octavo, cloth, 15s.

History of Nepāl, translated from the Original by MUNSHI SHEW SHUNKER SINGH and Pandit SHRĪ GUNĀNAND; edited with an Introductory Sketch of the Country and People by Dr D. WRIGHT, late Residency Surgeon at Kāthmāndū, and with numerous Illustrations and portraits of Sir JUNG BAHĀDUR, the King of Nepāl, and other natives. Super-Royal Octavo, 21s.

The University of Cambridge from the Earliest Times to the Royal Injunctions of 1535. By JAMES BASS MULLINGER, M.A. Demy 8vo. cloth (734 pp.), 12s.

London : Cambridge Warehouse, 17 Paternoster Row.

History of the College of St John the Evangelist, by THOMAS BAKER, B.D., Ejected Fellow. Edited by JOHN E. B. MAYOR, M.A., Fellow of St John's. Two Vols. Demy 8vo. 24s.

The Architectural History of the University and Colleges of Cambridge, by the late Professor WILLIS, M.A. With numerous Maps, Plans, and Illustrations. Continued to the present time, and edited by JOHN WILLIS CLARK, M.A., formerly Fellow of Trinity College, Cambridge. *[In the Press.*

CATALOGUES.

Catalogue of the Hebrew Manuscripts preserved in the University Library, Cambridge. By Dr S. M. SCHILLER-SZINESSY. Volume I. containing Section I. *The Holy Scriptures;* Section II. *Commentaries on the Bible.* Demy 8vo. 9s.

A Catalogue of the Manuscripts preserved in the Library of the University of Cambridge. Demy 8vo. 5 Vols. 10s. each.

Index to the Catalogue. Demy 8vo. 10s.

A Catalogue of Adversaria and printed books containing MS. notes, preserved in the Library of the University of Cambridge. 3s. 6d.

The Illuminated Manuscripts in the Library of the Fitzwilliam Museum, Cambridge, Catalogued with Descriptions, and an Introduction, by WILLIAM GEORGE SEARLE, M.A., late Fellow of Queens' College, and Vicar of Hockington, Cambridgeshire. 7s. 6d.

A Chronological List of the Graces, Documents, and other Papers in the University Registry which concern the University Library. Demy 8vo. 2s. 6d.

Catalogus Bibliothecæ Burckhardtianæ. Demy Quarto. 5s.

MISCELLANEOUS.

Statuta Academiæ Cantabrigiensis. Demy 8vo. 2s.

Ordinationes Academiæ Cantabrigiensis. New Edition. Demy 8vo., cloth. 3s. 6d.

Trusts, Statutes and Directions affecting (1) The Professorships of the University. (2) The Scholarships and Prizes. (3) Other Gifts and Endowments. Demy 8vo. 5s.

A Compendium of University Regulations, for the use of persons in Statu Pupillari. Demy 8vo. 6d.

London: Cambridge Warehouse, 17 *Paternoster Row.*

The Cambridge Bible for Schools.

GENERAL EDITOR: J. J. S. PEROWNE, D.D., DEAN OF
PETERBOROUGH.

THE want of an Annotated Edition of the BIBLE, in handy portions, suitable for school use, has long been felt.

In order to provide Text-books for School and Examination purposes, the CAMBRIDGE UNIVERSITY PRESS has arranged to publish the several books of the BIBLE in separate portions, at a moderate price, with introductions and explanatory notes.

Some of the books have already been undertaken by the following gentlemen:

Rev. A. CARR, M.A., *late Fellow of Oriel College, Oxford.*

Rev. T. K. CHEYNE, M.A., *Fellow of Balliol College, Oxford.*

Rev. S. COX, *Nottingham.*

Rev. A. B. DAVIDSON, D.D., *Prof. of Hebrew, Free Church Coll. Edinb.*

Rev. F. W. FARRAR, D.D., *Canon of Westminster.*

Rev. A. E. HUMPHREYS, M.A., *Fellow of Trinity College, Cambridge.*

Rev. A. F. KIRKPATRICK, M.A., *Fellow and Lecturer of Trinity College.*

Rev. J. J. LIAS, M.A., *Professor at St David's College, Lampeter.*

Rev. J. R. LUMBY, D.D., *Norrisian Professor of Divinity.*

Rev. G. F. MACLEAR, D.D., *Head Master of King's Coll. School, London.*

Rev. H. C. G. MOULE, M.A., *Fellow of Trinity College, Cambridge.*

Rev. W. F. MOULTON, D.D., *Head Master of the Leys School, Cambridge.*

Rev. E. H. PEROWNE, D.D., *Master of Corpus Christi College, Cambridge, Examining Chaplain to the Bishop of St Asaph.*

The Ven. T. T. PEROWNE, B.D., *Archdeacon of Norwich.*

Rev. A. PLUMMER, M.A., *Master of University College, Durham.*

Rev. E. H. PLUMPTRE, D.D., *Professor of Biblical Exegesis, King's College, London.*

Rev. W. SANDAY, D.D., *Principal of Bishop Hatfield Hall, Durham.*

Rev. W. SIMCOX, M.A., *Rector of Weyhill, Hants.*

Rev. ROBERTSON SMITH, M.A., *Professor of Hebrew, Aberdeen.*

Rev. A. W. STREANE, M.A., *Fellow of Corpus Christi College.*

Rev. H. W. WATKINS, M.A., *Warden of St Augustine's Coll. Canterbury.*

Rev. G. H. WHITAKER, M.A., *Fellow of St John's College, Cambridge; Honorary Chancellor of Truro Cathedral.*

Rev. C. WORDSWORTH, M.A., *Rector of Glaston, Rutland.*

London: Cambridge Warehouse, 17 Paternoster Row.

Now Ready.

THE BOOK OF JOSHUA. By the Rev. G. F. MACLEAR, D.D.
With Two Maps. Cloth. 2s. 6d.

THE BOOK OF JONAH. By Archdeacon PEROWNE.
With Two Maps. Cloth. 1s. 6d.

THE GOSPEL ACCORDING TO ST MATTHEW. By the
Rev. A. CARR, M.A. With Two Maps. Cloth. 2s. 6d.

THE GOSPEL ACCORDING TO ST MARK. By the Rev.
G. F. MACLEAR, D.D. With Two Maps. Cloth. 2s. 6d.

THE GOSPEL ACCORDING TO ST LUKE. By the Rev.
F. W. FARRAR, D.D. With Four Maps. Cloth. 4s. 6d.

THE ACTS OF THE APOSTLES. Part I., Chaps. I.—XIV.
By the Rev. Professor LUMBY, D.D. Cloth. 2s. 6d.

THE EPISTLE TO THE ROMANS. By the Rev. H. C. G.
MOULE, M.A. Cloth. 3s. 6d.

THE FIRST EPISTLE TO THE CORINTHIANS. By the
Rev. Prof. LIAS, M.A. With a Plan and Map. Cloth. 2s.

THE SECOND EPISTLE TO THE CORINTHIANS. By
the Rev. Prof. LIAS, M.A. With a Plan and Map. Cloth. 2s.

THE GENERAL EPISTLE OF ST JAMES. By the Rev.
E. H. PLUMPTRE, D.D. Cloth. 1s. 6d.

THE EPISTLES OF ST PETER AND ST JUDE. By the
Rev. E. H. PLUMPTRE, D.D. Cloth. 2s. 6d.

Preparing.

THE GOSPEL ACCORDING TO ST JOHN. By the Rev.
W. SANDAY, D.D., and the Rev. A. PLUMMER, M.A.

THE BOOK OF JEREMIAH. By the Rev. A. W. STREANE,
M.A. *[Nearly ready.*

THE FIRST BOOK OF SAMUEL. By the Rev. A. F.
KIRKPATRICK, M.A.

THE BOOKS OF HAGGAI AND ZECHARIAH. By
Archdeacon PEROWNE.

In Preparation.

THE CAMBRIDGE GREEK TESTAMENT
FOR SCHOOLS AND COLLEGES,

with a Revised Text, based on the most recent critical authorities, and
English Notes, prepared under the direction of the General Editor,
THE VERY REVEREND J. J. S. PEROWNE, D.D.,
DEAN OF PETERBOROUGH.

The books will be published separately, as in the Cambridge Bible for Schools.

London: Cambridge Warehouse, 17 *Paternoster Row.*

THE PITT PRESS SERIES.

ADAPTED TO THE USE OF STUDENTS PREPARING
FOR THE

UNIVERSITY LOCAL EXAMINATIONS,

AND THE HIGHER CLASSES OF SCHOOLS.

I. GREEK.

Luciani Somnium Charon Piscator et De Luctu. (*New Edition with Appendix.*) With English Notes, by W. E. HEITLAND, M.A., Fellow of St John's College, Cambridge. *Price 3s. 6d.*

The Anabasis of Xenophon, Book VI. With a Map and English Notes by ALFRED PRETOR, M.A., Fellow of St Catharine's College, Editor of Sophocles (Trachiniæ) and Persius. *Price 2s 6d.*

—— **Books I. III. IV. and V.** By the same Editor. *Price 2s. each.* **Book II.** *Price 2s. 6d.*

Agesilaus of Xenophon. The Text revised with Critical and Explanatory Notes, Introduction, Analysis, and Indices. By H. HAILSTONE, M.A., late Scholar of Peterhouse, Cambridge, Editor of Xenophon's Hellenics, etc. *Price 2s. 6d.*

Aristophanes—Ranae. With English Notes and Introduction by W. C. GREEN, M.A., Assistant Master at Rugby School. Cloth. *3s. 6d.*

Aristophanes—Aves. By the same Editor. *New Edition.* Cloth. *3s. 6d.*

Euripides. Hercules Furens. With Introduction, Notes and Analysis. By J. T. HUTCHINSON, B.A., Christ's College, and A. GRAY, B.A., Fellow of Jesus College, Cambridge. *Price 2s.*

II. LATIN.

M. T. Ciceronis de Amicitia. Edited by J. S. REID, M.L., Fellow of Gonville and Caius College, Cambridge. *Price 3s.*

M. T. Ciceronis de Senectute. Edited by J. S. REID, M.L, *Price 3s. 6d.*

P. Vergili Maronis Aeneidos Liber VII. Edited with Notes by A. SIDGWICK, M.A., Tutor of Corpus Christi College, Oxford. *Price 1s. 6d.*

—— **Books VI. VIII. X. XI. XII.** By the same Editor. *Price 1s. 6d. each.*

—— **Books VII. VIII.** bound in one volume. *Price 3s.*

—— **Books X. XI. XII.** bound in one volume. *Price 3s. 6d.*

London: Cambridge Warehouse, 17 *Paternoster Row.*

PITT PRESS SERIES (*continued*).

Quintus Curtius. A Portion of the History (Alexander in India). By W. E. HEITLAND, M.A., Fellow and Lecturer of St John's College, Cambridge, and T. E. RAVEN, B.A., Assistant Master in Sherborne School. With Two Maps. *Price 3s. 6d.*

Gai Iuli Caesaris de Bello Gallico Comment. I. II. With Maps and Notes by A. G. PESKETT, M.A. Fellow of Magdalene College, Cambridge. *Price 2s. 6d.*

Gai Iuli Caesaris de Bello Gallico Comment. IV., V., and Com. VII. By the same Editor. *Price 2s.* each.

P. Ovidii Nasonis Fastorum Liber VI. With Notes by A. SIDGWICK, M.A. Tutor of Corpus Christi College, Oxford. *Price 1s. 6d.*

M. T. Ciceronis Oratio pro Archia Poeta. By J. S. REID, M.L., Fellow of Gonville and Caius College, Cambridge. *Price 1s. 6d.*

M. T. Ciceronis pro L. Cornelio Balbo Oratio. By J. S. REID, M.L., Fellow of Gonville and Caius College. *Price 1s. 6d.*

Beda's Ecclesiastical History, Books III., IV., printed from the MS. in the Cambridge University Library. Edited, with a life, Notes, Glossary, Onomasticon, and Index, by J. E. B. MAYOR, M.A., Professor of Latin, and J. R. LUMBY, D.D., Norrisian Professor of Divinity. *Price 7s. 6d.*

M. T. Ciceronis in Q. Caecilium Divinatio et in C. Verrem Actio. With Notes by W. E. HEITLAND, M.A., and H. COWIE, M.A., Fellows of St John's Coll., Cambridge. *Price 3s.*

M. T. Ciceronis in Gaium Verrem Actio Prima. With Notes by H. COWIE, M.A., Fellow of St John's Coll. *Price 1s. 6d.*

M. T. Ciceronis Oratio pro L. Murena, with English Introduction and Notes. By W. E. HEITLAND, M.A., Fellow of St John's College, Cambridge. Second Edition. *Price 3s.*

M. T. Ciceronis Oratio pro Tito Annio Milone, with English Notes, &c., by the Rev. JOHN SMYTH PURTON, B.D., late Tutor of St Catharine's College. *Price 2s. 6d.*

M. Annaei Lucani Pharsaliae Liber Primus, with English Introduction and Notes by W. E. HEITLAND, M.A., and C. E. HASKINS, M.A., Fellows of St John's Coll., Cambridge. *1s. 6d.*

London: Cambridge Warehouse, 17 Paternoster Row.

PITT PRESS SERIES (*continued*).
III. FRENCH.

Histoire du Siècle de Louis XIV. par Voltaire. Chaps. I.—XIII. Edited with Notes Philological and Historical, Biographical and Geographical Indices, etc. by GUSTAVE MASSON, B.A. Univ. Gallic., Assistant Master of Harrow School, and G. W. PROTHERO, M.A., Fellow and Lecturer of King's College, Cambridge, Examiner for the Historical Tripos. *Price 2s. 6d.*

—— **Part II. Chaps. XIV.—XXIV.** By the same Editors. With Three Maps. *Price 2s. 6d.*

Le Verre D'Eau. A Comedy, by SCRIBE. With a Biographical Memoir, and Grammatical, Literary and Historical Notes, by C. COLBECK, M.A., late Fellow of Trinity College, Cambridge; Assistant Master at Harrow School. *Price 2s.*

M. Daru, par M. C. A. SAINTE-BEUVE (Causeries du Lundi, Vol. IX.). With Biographical Sketch of the Author, and Notes Philological and Historical. By GUSTAVE MASSON, B.A. Univ. Gallic., Assistant Master and Librarian, Harrow School. *Price 2s.*

La Suite du Menteur. A Comedy by P. CORNEILLE. With Notes Philological and Historical by the same. *Price 2s.*

La Jeune Sibérienne. Le Lépreux de la Cité D'Aoste. Tales by COUNT XAVIER DE MAISTRE. With Biographical Notices, Critical Appreciations, and Notes, by the same. *Price 2s.*

Le Directoire. (Considérations sur la Révolution Française. Troisième et quatrième parties.) Par MADAME LA BARONNE DE STAËL-HOLSTEIN. With Notes by the same. *Price 2s.*

Fredégonde et Brunehaut. A Tragedy in Five Acts, by N. LEMERCIER. With Notes by the same. *Price 2s.*

Dix Années d'Exil. Livre II. Chapitres 1—8. Par MADAME LA BARONNE DE STAËL-HOLSTEIN. With Notes Historical and Philological. By the same. *Price 2s.*

Le Vieux Célibataire. A Comedy, by COLLIN D'HARLEVILLE. With Notes, by the same. *Price 2s.*

La Métromanie, A Comedy, by PIRON, with Notes, by the same. *Price 2s.*

Lascaris, ou Les Grecs du XVᴱ Siècle, Nouvelle Historique, par A. F. VILLEMAIN, with a Selection of Poems on Greece, and Notes, by the same. *Price 2s.*

PITT PRESS SERIES (*continued*).
IV. GERMAN.

Hauff, Das Wirthshaus im Spessart. By A. SCHLOTTMANN, Ph.D., Assistant Master at Uppingham School. *Price 3s. 6d.*

Der Oberhof. A Tale of Westphalian Life, by KARL IMMERMANN. With a Life of Immermann and English Notes, by WILHELM WAGNER, Ph.D., Professor at the Johanneum, Hamburg. *Price 3s.*

A Book of German Dactylic Poetry. Arranged and Annotated by WILHELM WAGNER, Ph.D., Professor at the Johanneum, Hamburg. *Price 3s.*

Der erste Kreuzzug (1095—1099) nach FRIEDRICH VON RAUMER. THE FIRST CRUSADE. Arranged and Annotated by WILHELM WAGNER, Ph. D., Professor at the Johanneum, Hamburg. *Price 2s.*

A Book of Ballads on German History. Arranged and Annotated by WILHELM WAGNER, PH. D., Professor at the Johanneum, Hamburg. *Price 2s.*

Der Staat Friedrichs des Grossen. By G. FREYTAG. With Notes. By WILHELM WAGNER, PH. D. Professor at the Johanneum, Hamburg. *Price 2s.*

Goethe's Knabenjahre. (1749—1759.) Goethe's Boyhood: being the First Three Books of his Autobiography. Arranged and Annotated by the same Editor. *Price 2s.*

Goethe's Hermann and Dorothea. With an Introduction and Notes. By the same Editor. *Price 3s.*

Das Jahr 1813 (THE YEAR 1813), by F. KOHLRAUSCH. With English Notes by the same Editor. *Price 2s.*

V. ENGLISH.

The Two Noble Kinsmen, edited with Introduction and Notes by the Rev. Professor SKEAT, M.A., formerly Fellow of Christ's College, Cambridge. Cloth, extra fcap. 8vo. *Price 3s. 6d.*

Bacon's History of the Reign of King Henry VII. With Notes by the Rev. Professor LUMBY, D.D., Fellow of St Catharine's College. Cambridge. Cloth, extra fcap. 8vo. *Price 3s.*

Sir Thomas More's Utopia. With Notes by the Rev. Professor LUMBY, D.D. *Price 3s. 6d.*

Locke on Education. With Introduction and Notes by the Rev. R. H. QUICK, M.A. *Price 3s. 6d.*

Sir Thomas More's Life of Richard III. With Notes, &c., by Professor LUMBY. [*In Preparation.*

Other Volumes are in preparation.

UNIVERSITY OF CAMBRIDGE LOCAL EXAMINATIONS.

EXAMINATION PAPERS,

for various years, with the *Regulations for the Examination.*
Demy Octavo. 2*s.* each, or by Post 2*s.* 2*d.*

(*The Regulations for the Examination in* 1880 *are now ready.*)

CLASS LISTS FOR VARIOUS YEARS.

6*d.* each, by Post 7*d.* After 1877, Boys 1*s.* Girls 6*d.*

ANNUAL REPORTS OF THE SYNDICATE,

With Supplementary Tables showing the success and failure of the Candidates.

2*s.* each, by Post 2*s.* 2*d.*

HIGHER LOCAL EXAMINATIONS.

EXAMINATION PAPERS FOR 1879,

to which are added the Regulations for 1880.

Demy Octavo. 2*s.* each, by Post 2*s.* 2*d.*

REPORTS OF THE SYNDICATE.

Demy Octavo. 1*s.*, by Post 1*s.* 1*d.*

CAMBRIDGE UNIVERSITY REPORTER.

Published by Authority.

Containing all the Official Notices of the University, Reports of Discussions in the Schools, and Proceedings of the Cambridge Philosophical, Antiquarian, and Philological Societies. 3*d.* weekly.

CAMBRIDGE UNIVERSITY EXAMINATION PAPERS.

These Papers are published in occasional numbers every Term, and in volumes for the Academical year.

VOL. V.	Parts 41 to 55.	PAPERS for the Year	1875—6, 12*s. cloth.*
VOL. VI.	,, 56 to 69.	,,	,,	1876—7, 12*s. cloth.*
VOL. VII.	,, 70 to 86.	,,	,,	1877—8, 12*s. cloth.*
VOL. VIII.	,, 87 to 104.	,,	,,	1878—9, 12*s. cloth.*

London:

CAMBRIDGE WAREHOUSE, 17 PATERNOSTER ROW.

Cambridge: DEIGHTON, BELL AND CO.

Leipzig: F. A. BROCKHAUS.

CAMBRIDGE: PRINTED BY C. J. CLAY, M.A. AT THE UNIVERSITY PRESS.